The Best Bike Rides in the Pacific Northwest

"There is a thorough description for each ride. Authors . . . brief you . . . on the finer points of bicycle cruising."

—Touring America

"Offer[s] 50 rides ranging from alpine gaspers and groaners to soft-pedaled rambles. . . . This is for anyone who rides."

—The Oregonian

"Natives as well as visitors . . . will be treated to rides local cyclists have enjoyed for years. They're all here, accompanied by easy-to-use maps and a wealth of interesting stories."

—The Bicycle Paper

D0376984

Best Bike Rides Series

THE BEST BIKE RIDES IN THE PACIFIC NORTHWEST

British Columbia · Idaho Oregon · Washington

Second Edition

by
Todd Litman and Suzanne Kort

A Voyager Book

The Globe Pequot Press

Old Saybrook, Connecticut

Library of Congress Cataloging-in-Publication Data
Litman, Todd.
    The best bike rides in the Pacific Northwest: British Columbia, Idaho, Oregon, and Washington / by Todd Litman and Suzanne Kort. — 2nd ed.
        p   cm. — (Best bike rides series)
"A voyager book."
Includes appendix.
ISBN 1-56440-750-0
    1. Bicycle touring—Northwest, Pacific—Guide-books. 2. Northwest, Pacific—Guidebooks. I. Kort, Suzanne. II. Title. III. Series.
GV1045.5.N67L58 1996
796.6'4'09795—dc20   95-39188
                                                                    CIP

♻ This book is printed on recycled paper.
Manufactured in the United States of America
Second Edition/Second Printing

Bicycling in the magnificent Pacific Northwest has helped us appreciate life's simple pleasures: the beauty of rural landscapes, the fun of exploring new places and making friends along the way, the satisfaction of traveling under one's own power, the gratification of good food after healthy outdoor exercise. We are delighted to share such joys with our readers.

We wish that everybody had opportunities for such pleasures. It is sad that some people cannot afford even the simple enjoyment of recreational bicycling. It would be tragic if future generations could not bicycle through quiet forests, healthy farmlands, and spectacular wildlands as we do now.

We believe that bicycling offers an opportunity to share the world's resources more fairly and to preserve some of our planet's best features, such as fresh air, clean water, and healthy living things. We therefore dedicate this book to people who make an effort to bicycle more and drive less. We would especially like to recognize the important efforts of organizations such as the Institute for Transportation and Development Policy, the Worldwatch Institute, and the League of American Bicyclists to encourage and support bicycle transportation. Finally, we would like to thank our parents, who allowed us to explore the world at our own pace.

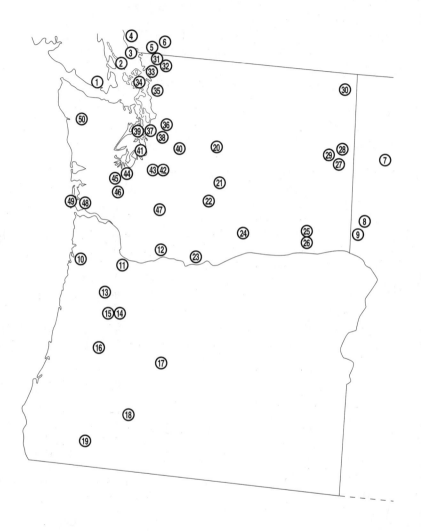

Contents

Introduction

The Pacific Northwest offers some of the most enjoyable bicycling found anywhere in the world. This book is an overview of some of our region's best bicycling. Most rides included here are based on routes used by bicycle organizations for organized events such as club "century" rides. You may be inspired to participate in these events, or you can use the directions in this book to ride the routes on your own. Either way, the rides included here offer delightful bicycling adventures.

Whether you prefer easy rides, challenging rides, or rides that include fun activities in addition to bicycling, you'll find many excellent opportunities in our region. The Pacific Northwest, including Oregon, Idaho, Washington, and southwest British Columbia, is a diverse region of cities, farm valleys, mountains, islands, deserts, rivers, ocean coasts, and forests. These rides enable you to enjoy each of these environments. We also provide information about museums, parks, and other attractions along the way to add to your enjoyment. There are few better ways to explore our region than by bicycle.

Here are examples of rides you will find described in this book:

• The Crater Lake Challenge circles one of the world's most beautiful and dramatic natural structures, the sparkling blue lake in Mount Mazama's volcanic crater.

• The King County Trail Ramble connects urban Seattle with rural parks and wineries, offering up to 51 miles of riding with no competing motor vehicle traffic.

• The Carson Hot Springs Challenge rides make an ideal two-day trip through the magnificent Columbia River Gorge, from Portland to the historic Carson Hot Mineral Springs Resort and back, nourishing both the body and the soul.

• Several rides in Puget Sound, San Juan, and Gulf Islands combine delightful bicycling with spectacular ferry rides and sightseeing opportunities.

How to Use This Book

This book features 50 recommended bicycle rides, with information to help you prepare for your trip and easily navigate the routes. Ride descriptions include maps, directions, altitude profiles, and help in getting started, finding food, and obtaining more information. You'll also learn about historical highlights, tourist activities, and other background about the areas through which you will ride.

To help select routes suitable for your riding abilities and style, rides are named to reflect four degrees of difficulty:

Rambles are the easiest rides, suitable for beginners and cyclists looking for relaxed outings. Rambles range from about 10 to 35 miles in length over relatively flat courses.

Cruises are intermediate-level rides from 25 to 60 miles in length. They often include a few hills.

Challenges are for riders who are adequately prepared. Most of these rides are more than 50 miles in length and may include significant climbs.

Classics are the most difficult of the rides presented here, suitable for strong and experienced riders. They range from 75 to more than 100 miles in length and include major climbs.

Within this structure you will find considerable flexibility. We think of the routes presented here the way a jazz musician thinks of a melody; they are the basic structures from which endless variations can be improvised. You will notice that most ride descriptions include suggestions for shorter or longer options of the primary route. As you become confident with your riding and navigation abilities, you will find that you can develop variations of your own. By all means do; exploring "uncharted" roads offers additional adventures and allows you to modify a route to meet specific needs.

Use common sense to plan your rides to avoid traffic and road conditions that you would find unpleasant. It is important to be aware of *when* you ride, since conditions change depending on time of day, day of the week, season of year, and weather. For example, many suburban roads and highways are most pleasant for .

bicycling weekends and in the middle of a weekday, but can be congested and unpleasant during rush hours. Similarly, many scenic highways are crowded with motor homes and other tourist vehicles during summer months; you may prefer to ride a little off-season, or put in some relaxing miles early in the day while most tourists are still in camp. Of course, heavy rain, high winds, and darkness are especially difficult and dangerous. Only experienced and well-equipped cyclists should ride these routes under such conditions.

We recommend that you carry a road map of the area in addition to the route map included in this book, especially if you are unfamiliar with the territory. There are several reasons for this: You may want additional geographic information to satisfy your curiosity about the area, you may need to find your way around an unexpected barrier (such as a road closure), or you may want to modify the route for other reasons. A road map also helps navigate if for some reason you get totally lost, if road names have changed, or if, heaven forbid, a route description in this book is unclear.

Tips for Enjoyable Bicycling

Bicycling can be safe, enjoyable, and rewarding if you are prepared. Here is our advice for trouble-free riding:

Riding skills. Before embarking on any of these rides, you should have sufficient bicycle-handling skills to maneuver through light traffic, use your bicycle's gears and brakes, and avoid hazards. For information on bicycling skills we recommend the excellent booklet *Street Smarts,* by John Allen (available for $1 from the publishers of *Bicycling Magazine,* Rodale Press, 33 E. Minor, Emmaus, PA 18098, (610) 967–5171); or take an Effective Cycling training course if one is available in your community. Check with your bike club, recreation department, or local college for information about such courses. You can also get advice and encouragement by participating in rides sponsored by your local bike club.

Develop a smooth and efficient pedaling technique. This means using your gears to maintain a high (60–90 rpm) cadence. Beginning riders often push too hard in a high gear. Toe clips (or clipless pedals) and cycling shoes allow you to pedal faster, easier, and with greater efficiency. Good pedaling technique reduces your chances of straining your muscles or joints, provides a more efficient workout, and allows you to ride longer without getting tired. Try to relax as you ride. Keep your elbows bent, and alternate regularly between various handlebar positions. Breathe deeply, especially while climbing. On long climbs alternate between pedaling from a sitting position and standing on the pedals.

Practice emergency braking, using both brakes and moving back and low on the bicycle to put weight on the rear wheel. Also practice avoiding rocks and potholes in the roadway without swerving into another lane. Slow down, and take special care when approaching rough or slippery surfaces; gravel, potholes, wet surfaces, cracks in the roadway, and railroad tracks are some of the most common causes of bicycle accidents. Avoid sudden turns or braking on wet or gravel surfaces.

Cross railroad tracks and cracks in the roadway at as close to a right angle as possible to avoid getting your wheel caught. When riding over rough pavement, stand up on your pedals and absorb the shock in your arms and legs. Practice these avoidance maneuvers, and don't be afraid to walk your bicycle through hazardous conditions: Accident prevention is better than any cure.

Traffic rules and courtesy. Roadway traffic is a complex dance that depends on all participants following the choreography. Bicyclists have a proper place in this dance; it is important to know your rights and responsibilities and behave courteously to other road users. By riding responsibly you help all bicyclists earn the respect of drivers.

Generally, bicyclists follow the same traffic laws as other drivers: Ride on the right side of the roadway, obey traffic signs and signals, yield when required. Bicyclists should be especially familiar with the rules that apply to slow vehicles: Slower bicyclists should stay near the right side of the roadway to facilitate faster vehicles passing. It is sometimes possible to ride on the road shoulder, but often bicycling is easier and safer when riding just left of the fog line that marks the right edge of the traffic lane.

Getting fit. You need two types of training to maximize your enjoyment of bicycling. First, an aerobic foundation allows your heart and lungs to work long hours. To establish this foundation exercise at least twenty minutes at a time, at least three days a week. Bicycling, fast walking, jogging, swimming, or other active sports can all provide an aerobic workout. Second, you need "butt miles," enough bicycling to develop muscles, calluses, and confidence. Ride at least twice a week, slowly increasing your distance.

Even better is to integrate bicycling into your daily life. Ride to work, on errands, and as a social activity. This provides multiple benefits: You maintain your training while reducing pollution, petroleum use, and travel costs. Replacing automobile use with bicycling allows you to fit exercise into a busy schedule and contribute toward a better world.

Pacing. You will enjoy bicycling more if you pace yourself. On longer rides start out slowly, and settle into a steady pace as you warm up. Take time to rest, stretch, and explore sights along the way. Drink and eat enough to maintain your energy. Most organized bicycling events provide refreshments, but carry a little extra food and drink as a backup. Be sure to bring plenty of water on rides with long distances between reliable supplies; you can get mighty thirsty over a 20- or 30-mile stretch.

If you are new to bicycling, be sure to work up to longer distances gradually. Choose the easier "Rambles" before trying a "Cruise" or "Classic." Bicycling is usually most enjoyable if you schedule enough time off your bike to rest and explore along the way. Your fondest memory from a bicycle trip often turns out to be something other than riding: a leisurely picnic, touring a small museum, or an enlightening conversation with local residents.

Bicycling in groups. Riding in a group requires special care. Each rider should share the responsibility for avoiding hazards and being courteous to other road users. When bicycling at relatively low speeds on low-traffic roads, road shoulders, and trails, it is often possible to ride side by side. When traffic approaches from behind, or for more efficient riding, form a single pace line toward the right side of the roadway. The front rider in a pace line must work harder to overcome wind resistance, so riders often take turns, typically falling to the back of the line after taking a five- to ten-minute "pull."

Keep groups small—six riders is usually a good maximum—to allow other vehicles to pass easily. A pace line is especially difficult to maintain on a narrow, crowded, and curvy highway; be prepared to break into smaller groups when required for safety. Experienced riders often stay just a few inches apart, but this requires concentration and experience. If in doubt back off a little. When riding in a pace line, call a warning, and point out rocks, potholes, or other hazards in the roadway to the riders behind. It is important that each rider in a group signal and yield when required while making a turn or when stopping. When the group stops to rest, all riders should get off the roadway completely to avoid blocking traffic.

Equipment. It is not necessary to have an expensive bicycle to enjoy riding. It is important, though, that your bicycle be properly maintained. Check tires, wheels, brakes, and drivetrain before each ride. If you are not sure how to check or maintain your bicycle, get advice through a friendly bike shop, your local bike club, or a bicycle-repair book. Some community-education programs offer bicycle maintenance courses for beginners; this can be an excellent investment.

Adjust your bicycle for proper fit. The bike frame should be the correct size, allowing you to comfortably straddle the top tube when standing. The seat should be adjusted to the proper height and angle, so your legs maintain a slight bend at the bottom of the pedal stroke. If your hips rock as you pedal, the seat is probably too high. Handlebar position, toe-clip size, and even brake-levers size can be adjusted for fit. Consult a reliable bike shop for advice and help.

Your choice of bicycling accessories is almost as important as your selection of a bicycle. Accessories modify your bicycle to match your particular needs. A cyclometer helps you navigate. A small handlebar or seat bag is useful for carrying tools, food, and extra clothes. A pump and repair kit are important if you will be riding on your own. A rack, water bottle, lock, and light make your bicycle more useful. We recommend that you install fenders on your bicycle; they double the number of days that you can comfortably ride here in the damp Pacific Northwest. A helmet protects the most valuable component on your bicycle.

Learn to fix a flat tire and make minor adjustments before touring on your own. Be prepared: This means carrying a spare tube, repair kit, and basic tools that match your bicycle's components. A small roll of plastic electrical tape can solve many problems. Always take extra money and identification for emergencies.

Dress for bicycling. Cycling clothing is designed for comfort, efficiency, and safety, and it is now available in a wide variety of styles to satisfy any taste. Although specialized clothing is not absolutely necessary, it greatly increases your enjoyment, especially if you ride long distances or in adverse conditions. Jerseys and shorts are cut to fit properly when you ride, prevent chafing, and minimize wind resistance. Shorts have a padded lining (since the lining is designed to contact skin, don't wear underwear beneath bicycling shorts). Cycling gloves are padded and allow ventilation. Cycling shoes have a stiff sole for efficient pedaling and are designed to fit toe clips or clipless pedals. Tights and cycling jackets keep you warm under cold and wet conditions without restricting movement or making you too hot.

Carry an extra layer of clothing when bicycling—Pacific Northwest weather can change suddenly, even during the summer.

Publications and clubs. We are lucky to have two excellent regional bicycling publications in the Pacific Northwest: *Oregon Cycling* and *The Bicycle Paper*. Both include excellent calendars of bicycling activities and events. We recommend that you subscribe to at least one.

Joining a local bicycle club allows you to support and participate in a variety of bicycling activities. Whether your interest is recreational riding, touring, racing, or promoting bicycle transportation, your bicycle club can help. Through your local club you can meet wonderful people, learn more about our sport, and contribute to your community. Club-sponsored rides provide an excellent opportunity to develop your riding technique with the help of experienced riders. Bicycle clubs rely on volunteers like yourself to run events such as those described in this book and to provide a variety of community services.

Our national bicycling organizations provide important support for bicycling. These include the League of American Bicyclists, the largest general interest bicycling organization; Bikecentennial, an organization that supports long-distance bicycle touring; the United States Cycling Federation, our national amateur bicycle-racing organization; and the Bicycle Federation of America, a professional organization for bicycle advocates and planners.

See the Appendix for addresses for the organizations described above.

Disclaimer

The Globe Pequot Press assumes no liability for accidents happening to, or injuries sustained by, readers who engage in the activities described in this book.

British Columbia

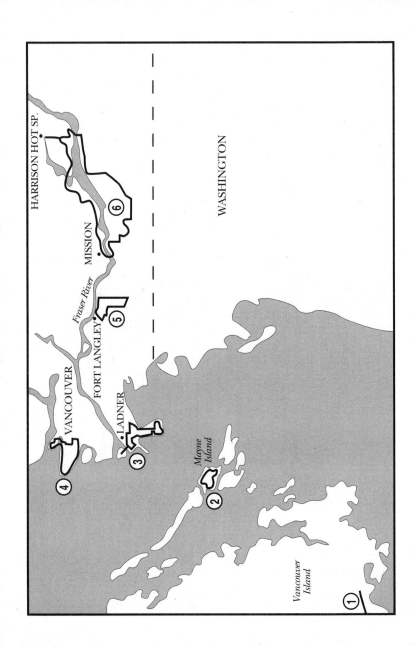

British Columbia

Note: Telephone area codes on Vancouver and Mayne Islands change from 604 to 250 after October 1996. Prior to that date, use 604 for all areas of British Columbia.

1

Galloping Goose Ramble

Atkins Avenue—Galloping Goose Trail—Roche Cove

Advertisers of products from candy to life insurance love using photos of bicyclists riding forest trails with brilliant sunlight filtering through vibrantly colored leaves. This idyllic image conveys healthy, outdoor fun removed from the stresses of civilization. The Galloping Goose Trail, outside Victoria on Vancouver Island, really offers this kind of bicycling experience. It is one of many trails that have been developed from abandoned railroad rights-of-way as part of the "rails-to-trails" movement. It bears the popular name of the rickety old railroad that once connected isolated logging communities with the city of Victoria.

Like other trails developed on railroad beds, the Galloping Goose has no steep inclines. The beautiful 15-mile stretch described here meanders through forests, with a scattering of small farms and occasional glimpses of the Strait of Juan de Fuca and the Olympic Mountains beyond. It has a well-maintained gravel surface suitable for mountain or touring bicycles (but a little rough for racing bikes). Most of the ride is completely separated from any roadway. You'll hear the chirping of birds and smell the intoxicating aroma of forests rather than the sounds and smells of automobile traffic.

Since this is a mixed-use trail, you'll be sharing it with pedestrians and equestrians. Please show consideration by slowing down when you approach other trail users, giving a polite warning before you pass from behind, and yielding when necessary. Be especially careful to avoid spooking horses with threatening or unexpected moves.

The route described here, from Atkins Avenue to Roche Cove Regional Park, is one of the most pleasant stretches of the trail's approximately 40-mile length. If you have the time, you can continue for another 6 miles along the shoreline for a visit to the town of Sooke or travel all of the way up the Sooke River Canyon, past the river's potholes, to the abandoned logging community of Leechtown. You'll find stores, restaurants, and a historical museum in Sooke, but you'll need to carry supplies if you continue up the Canyon.

The trail is being extended and may connect with downtown Victoria by the time you read this. If this ride whets your appetite for public trails in your own community, you may want to contact the Rails-to-Trails Conservancy (1400 Sixteenth Street NW, Washington, D.C. 20036; 202–797–5400), which promotes the development of trails from abandoned railroad corridors. They can provide information on other trails in your area as well as rail-to-trail projects you can support.

The Basics

Start: Atkins Ave., just off the Island Hwy. (1A) in View Royal, about 4 miles west of downtown Victoria. Public parking is available there. The official trailhead is in Victoria at the west end of the Johnson St. Bridge. Parts of the trail between Victoria and View Royal may still be under development.

Length: 31 miles total round-trip. There are shorter and longer options on the trail, or you can circle back from Roche Cove by road.

Terrain: Although the region is hilly, the trail is nearly flat. It has a well-maintained gravel surface suitable for any bike with medium or large cross-section tires.

Food: A gas station and convenience store is just down the highway from the starting point, and you'll find stores and restaurants along the highway at 2 miles and 4.7 miles. Bring sufficient food and water if you plan to ride the entire route. You'll find a conve-

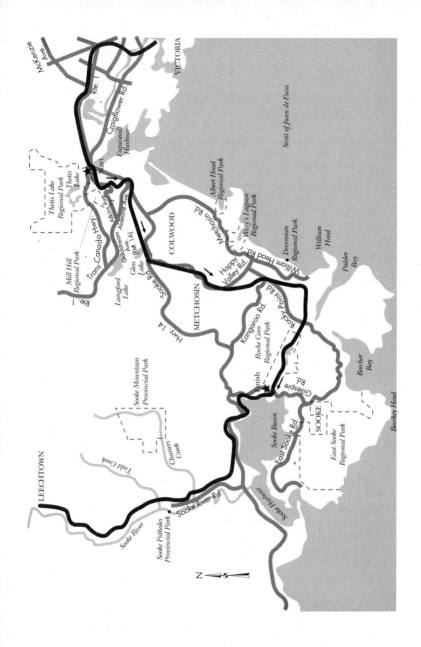

nience store on Sooke Rd., 3 miles past Roche Cove, and there are store and restaurants in Sooke.

For more information: Capital Regional District Parks, (250) 474–7275 or (250) 478–3344.

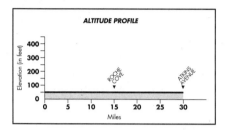

Miles and Directions

- 0.0 Head west from Atkins Ave. (left if your back is to the highway).
- 1.7 Turn right onto the Island Hwy. (also called Sooke Rd. at this point). Since it is a busy highway, you may choose to ride on the sidewalk rather than the roadway. An alternative route is to cross the highway (carefully!) and take the short loop of trail that circles back to the highway, which you'll have to cross again.
- 2.3 Turn right onto Aldeane Ave. Pick up the Galloping Goose Trail here.
- 4.7 Cross Sooke Rd.
- 13.1 Matheson Lake Park. Hiking trail and public toilets to your left.
- 15.5 Roche Cove Park parking lot. Turn around here, or cross Gillespie Rd. and continue 2.7 miles on the trail to Sooke Rd. There you can either turn left for a 3-mile ride to Sooke, or cross the highway and ride another 10 miles up the Sooke River Canyon to Leechtown.

2

Mayne Island Ramble

Village Bay—Miners Bay—Campbell Bay
Piggot Bay—Dinner Bay—Village Bay

All the Gulf Islands offer pleasurable riding, but Mayne is especially popular with recreational bicyclists. There is plenty to see on this island, and .the roads form a nice loop. Although the basic route is less than 13 miles, few riders complain that there isn't enough to do during their time on the island.

The loop circling Mayne Island is the starting point for side trips to quiet bays, beaches, and windy points of land, each offering a unique view of the beautiful waters and islands of the Strait of Georgia. Art galleries on the island display the creative work of the many artists who call Mayne their home. There is so much to do here that many cyclists opt for an extended stay. Mayne has resorts and bed-and-breakfast guest houses, where cyclists often stay. These are especially busy during the summer months, when vacationers flock to the islands, so make reservations early if possible.

Mayne Island is easily accessible from both the mainland and Vancouver Island. The ferry ride, about one hour each way, offers time to relax and take in the view. Visitors to Mayne must stay at least six hours, since there is only one ferry arriving in the morning and another in the late afternoon. The ferry schedule varies, depending on the season and day of the week. For information call the Vancouver BC Ferries office at (604) 685–1021 or the Swartz Bay/Victoria office at (250) 656–0757.

You'll arrive at the public ferry dock in Village Bay. It's best to wait at the terminal until most automobile traffic has passed;

you'll have the roadway largely to yourself as you ride to the island's business district, a small group of shops at Miners Bay. Depending on your tastes you can sample a meal at The Mayne Mast Restaurant, stop for a beer at the Springwater Lodge bar, snack at the Miners Bay Deli, or just stock up at one of the two stores in "town." You might also stop at the Mayne Museum in the old (1896) Plumper Pass jail building to learn more about the island's unique history.

Follow Georgina Point Road to the Active Pass Light Station. Visitors are welcome from 1:00 to 3:00 P.M. There you can learn about the stalwart lighthouses that have stood at this location since 1885 and enjoy spectacular views north up the Strait of Georgia. Looking west, you may catch a glimpse of killer whales playing in the waves of Active Pass. You'll then follow Waugh Road to Campbell Bay. Down a short, narrow path is a public beach where local residents often take a swim.

Follow Campbell Bay Road to Fernhill Road. If your schedule allows, you may want to stop at Bennett Bay, Horton Bay (both of which offer magnificent views of the Strait of Georgia), or the swimming beach at Piggot Bay. There is also a county park at Dinner Bay, 2 miles from the ferry dock, an ideal place to rest if you still have extra time before your ferry leaves.

For a different type of adventure, consider hiking the secluded forest trail to Helen Point, a 5-mile round-trip. The trailhead is marked by a small sign on a telephone pole, .8 miles from the ferry terminal on Village Bay Road.

Mayne makes a good base camp for day trips to other islands, including Galiano, Pender, Saltspring, and Saturna. For an especially enjoyable ride, follow East Point Road on Saturna Island to its end, opposite Tumbo Island. This 20-mile round-trip route along a beautiful public beach has wonderful views and light traffic.

The Basics

Start: Mayne Island ferry dock. From the mainland, take the Tsawwassen ferry (20 miles south of Vancouver). From Vancouver

Island, take the Swartz Bay ferry.

Length: 12.7 miles, with numerous side trips.

Terrain: Hilly, narrow roads, light traffic.

Food: Two restaurants (The Mayne Mast and Springwater Inn), two grocery stores (Mayne Open Market and The Trading Post), the Trincomali Bakery, and the Miners Bay Deli can be found in Miners Bay, at 1.5 miles. The Centre Stop, a small store, is at 7.0 miles; and nearby is the Fernhill Lodge, at 7.2 miles, which offers fine dining.

For more information: British Columbia Tourist Information, (800) 663–6000.

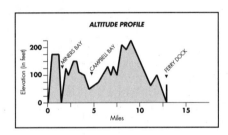

Miles & Directions

- 0.0 Turn left from the Mayne Island ferry dock parking lot to follow Village Bay Rd. up the hill.
- 1.5 Miners Bay, the commercial center of Mayne Island. Turn left onto Fernhill Rd., then right onto Georgina Pt. Rd.
- 3.3 Right onto Waugh Rd.

    To the left 0.5 mile farther is the Active Pass Lighthouse at the end of Georgina Point.

- 4.8 Bear right at intersection with Porter Rd.
- 5.2 Campbell Bay. To get down to the beach, follow the narrow trail that begins between the first and second warning arrow signs at the approach to the bay.
- 6.4 Turn left onto Fernhill Rd.

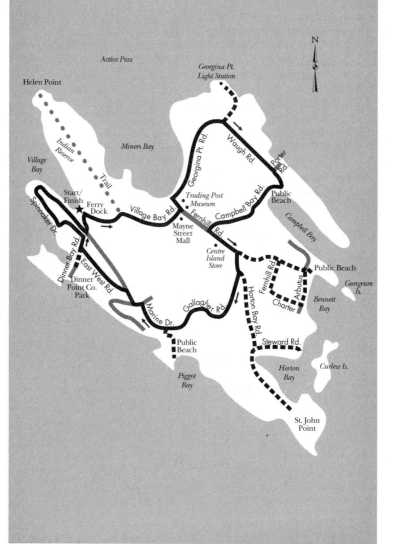

- 7.0 Centre Stop store.
- 7.1 Turn right onto Horton Bay Rd. To the left 1.2 miles on Fernhill Rd. is Bennett Bay.
- 7.5 Turn right on Gallagher Rd. To the left 1.5 miles is Horton Bay, with public beach access at the end of Steward Rd.
- 8.9 Bear right onto Marine Dr. To the left 0.5 miles is Piggot Bay.
- 9.1 Follow Marine Dr. left.
- 9.2 Bear right onto Mainers Way.
- 9.7 Turn left onto East West Rd.
- 10.8 Turn right onto Dinner Bay Rd. At 0.5 miles to the left is Dinner Bay County Park.
- 10.9 Continue straight onto Spinnaker Dr.
- 11.6 Follow Spinnaker Dr. as it curves right.
- 12.2 Turn left on Dalton Dr.
- 12.7 End back at ferry dock.

3

Point Roberts Cruise

Westham Island—Point Roberts
Boundary Bay—Tsawwassen—Ladner

A coyote traverses the beach in the distance, shorebirds call as they busily poke the sand for food, red-winged blackbirds sing love songs along the reedy shore. The joys of nature are a bicycle length away on this pleasant international cruise, a popular ride among members of the Vancouver Bicycle Club.

Plan to visit the Reifel Wildlife Sanctuary either at the start or end of your tour. Located in an estuarine marsh, the sanctuary sustains the largest population of wintering waterfowl in Canada. Birds start arriving in August, and their numbers reach a peak by November. While many return north in March, May and June are still the best times to see the ducklings and goslings of the year-round residents. Even if you don't have time to hike the paths under the wings of raptors and snow geese, you might catch a glimpse of the pet sandhill crane standing several feet tall at the sanctuary entrance or view mallards and sandpipers nearby.

Heading south over Westham Island and across the one-lane bridge, you'll begin exploring the rural delta landscape. Here at the mouth of the Fraser River, the influence of the sea is never far away. Salty air, careening gulls, glimpses of fishing boats and nets will tickle your senses as you head west along River Road toward the Strait of Georgia.

Once on the dike at the end of River Road, you can enjoy the pleasure of riding away from traffic along a beautiful stretch of shore. Your eyes can feast on views of distant island silhouettes and playful birds exploring the rich estuary. At the end of this stretch you will pass near the long Roberts Bank Coal Port spit, where coal from the mountains of Canada are shipped to furnaces in Japan.

Traveling south, rural roads take you through residential Tsawwassen. English Bluff Road, lined with private homes, skirts a cliff overlooking the Strait of Georgia, offering an occasional glimpse of the sea. Better vistas await you on the less inhabited shoreline south of the border.

After Customs, Roosevelt Way takes you west along a narrow ditch that marks the Canada–U.S. border. To your right is a crowded Canadian neighborhood. The wooded areas to your left mark the uniqueness of Point Roberts: an American outpost cut off from the rest of the country by 25 miles of friendly but foreign land. At the end of Roosevelt Way, you will find a 19-foot obelisk overlooking the sea. Imported from Scotland in 1861, this structure marks the western end of the British Columbia–Washington border.

Follow the shoreline to the south end of Point Roberts peninsula, then east to Boundary Bay. Tourist beaches, Lighthouse County Park, and the Point Roberts Marina can be explored along the way. On this part of the trip you'll see beachfront summer homes and yachts. Back across the border you'll pass through the commercial center of busy Tsawwassen, then follow the shoreline for another enchanting oceanside ride atop a dike. Turning inland across the rich delta farmlands covered with vegetable, flower, and livestock farms, you'll work your way back to the wildlife sanctuary.

The Basics

Start: Reifel Wildlife Sanctuary parking lot. From Vancouver, follow Hwy. 99 south. Take the Ladner Centre exit, just past the George Massey Tunnel. Follow River Rd. 2 miles west to the town of Ladner. Turn left at T onto Elliot Ave., then right at the light onto Ladner Trunk Rd., which becomes River Rd. west. Follow this 2.4 miles west until you see a small yellow sign for the Reifel Sanctuary. Turn right onto Westham Rd., across the one-lane bridge onto Westham Island. Follow signs 3 miles to Reifel Sanctuary. Turn left at entrance to main parking lot.

Length: 38 miles.

Terrain: Mostly flat delta farmland. Some minor hills, especially at Point Roberts. Two lengths of excellent gravel dike road, approximately 2 miles each.

Food: Deltaport Farms fruit market at 9.4 miles; restaurants in Point Roberts, at 17.2 miles; Clarks Store at 21.2 miles, and many options in Tsawwassen at 25 miles.

For more information: Delta Chamber of Commerce Tourist Information, 6201 60th Ave., Delta, B.C. V4K 4E2; (604) 946–4232.

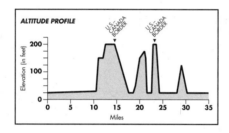

Miles & Directions

- 0.0 Follow driveway out of Reifel Sanctuary onto Robertson Rd. Robertson turns left to become Westham Island Rd. Follow this road as it curves left, then right, past berry farms and a nursery.
- 3.0 Cross bridge to mainland, then turn right onto River Rd.
- 4.8 River Rd. ends. Follow gravel road onto the river dike and continue west.
- 7.3 Dike road ends. Go around gate, and turn left onto 27B Ave. This takes a jog and becomes 28th Ave.
- 9.4 Turn right onto 52nd St.
- 10.5 Cross Hwy. 17, pass a golf course to your right, then climb a short, steep incline.

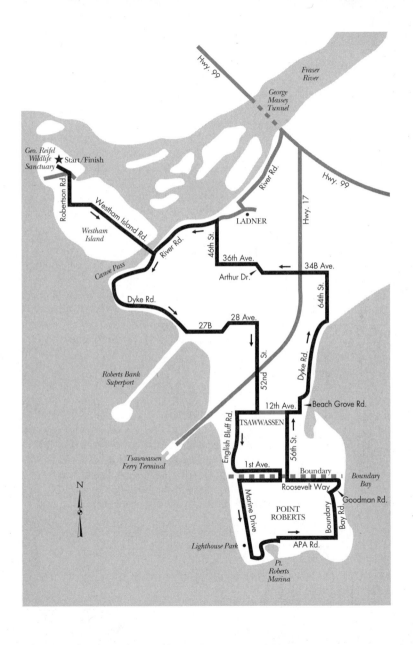

- 11.4 Turn right onto 12th Ave.
- 12.0 Turn left onto English Bluff Rd.
- 13.3 Turn left onto 1st Ave.
- 14.3 Turn right onto 56th St.
- 14.5 Cross border. Go through U.S. customs, then backtrack a few yards to follow Roosevelt Way west. The ditch to your right is the U.S.–Canada boundary. Granite obelisks mark the 48th Parallel border.
- 15.1 Turn left onto Marine Dr.
- 17.0 Cross Gulf Rd.
- 17.7 Lighthouse County Park is to your right.
- 18.0 Follow the road left around the Pt. Roberts Marina.
- 18.5 Turn right onto APA Rd.
- 20.2 Follow road left as it becomes Boundary Bay Rd.
- 21.2 Follow road as it curves left and then right onto Goodman Rd. This descends to the beach at Boundary Bay.
- 21.5 Turn left onto Bayview Dr.
- 21.7 Turn left back onto Roosevelt Way, along the Canadian border. Return to the customs station.
- 23.3 Turn right, cross border back into Canada. Continue north on Pt. Roberts Rd./56th St.
- 24.8 Turn right onto 12th Ave.
- 25.3 Turn left onto Beach Grove Rd. Follow this north through a residential neighborhood.
- 26.0 Where the road ends turn right onto a path to the beach. Follow this left, northward, along the dike road.
- 27.3 Pass through a gate, then turn left onto 64th St.
- 28.5 Turn left onto 34B Ave., and cross over Hwy. 17.
- 30.0 Turn right onto Arthur Dr., then take the next left onto 36th Ave., a low-traffic rural roadway.
- 31.3 Turn right onto 46th St.
- 33.0 Turn left onto River Rd. west.
- 34.8 Turn right onto Westham Island Rd. Cross bridge, and follow road back to Reifel Sanctuary.
- 37.5 Enter sanctuary, turn left along main drive.
- 38.0 End in sanctuary parking lot.

4

Vancouver Parks Ramble

Stanley Park—Spanish Banks
Southlands—Downtown

This urban ride explores some of Vancouver's highlights, including Stanley Park, beaches, the University of British Columbia, the Fraser River waterfront, and several lovely neighborhoods. It is a modified version of the route used in the Ride for Heart fundraiser and takes advantage of the Seaside Bike Route, developed by the city of Vancouver. If you are new to Vancouver, leave yourself plenty of time for this ride because there is much you'll want to stop and see.

Vancouver, British Columbia, is one of North America's most livable cities. The region is lush and beautiful, located between ocean and mountains, with a mild climate and abundant rainfall. This culturally and ethnically diverse community offers lots to explore. In a short time you are likely to encounter people of European, Oriental, Latin, Mid-Eastern, African, and Native American backgrounds and many opportunities to enjoy their food and cultural events. Vancouver is a people-oriented city with cohesive neighborhoods, a diversified transportation system, and outstanding urban parks. Cities facing urban decay and sprawl could learn much from this Pacific Northwest jewel.

This ride begins by circling Stanley Park, unique for its assortment of activities and old-growth evergreen forests. Within the park you can examine totem poles, see a cricket match, visit the zoo, ride a miniature train, and enjoy miles of public beaches.

There is more than enough to explore in just one visit.

Leaving Stanley Park you pass through downtown Vancouver and then cross False Creek on the Burrard Bridge. Across the bridge you'll pass the Centennial Museum, MacMillan Planetarium, and Maritime Museum and follow the waterfront along Kitsilano Beach Park. From there you can either take the bike route along 3rd Avenue, a quiet residential street, or ride on Cornwall, a busy artery. Both end at Jericho Beach Park. Following the path along the beach, you'll pass a colorful stream of bicyclists, in-line skaters, and pedestrians. Small sailboats and sailboards circle the bay while kites fly on the ocean breeze coming off the water.

Past Jericho Beach is Spanish Banks, a public beach that offers views of Lighthouse Park and Bowen Island to the north and the Strait of Georgia to the west. You'll climb toward the evergreen forests of Pacific Spirit Park. This park and wildlife sanctuary, originally part of the university's endowment land, has more than 50 kilometers of public trails, some suitable for mountain bike riding.

Across from the university is the Vancouver Museum of Anthropology, housing one of the world's finest collections of Northwest Indian artifacts, exquisitely displayed. Totem poles, standing in a specially constructed glass-walled building, look proudly out over the strait. Thousands of native tools and art objects provide a glimpse of prehistoric daily life.

Continue on Marine Drive through the university campus and along the cliffs above the Fraser River. Follow a gravel bridle path for a short distance along the Fraser River, and cross the Southlands, a community of riding clubs and stables. The route then turns north, passing through the beautiful gardens of Queen Elizabeth Park, around The Crescent, and charming residential neighborhoods with tree-lined streets that make Vancouver so livable. A few miles before returning to Stanley Park, you can stop at the shops and parks on Granville Island. Just take the .5-mile detour under the Granville Bridge to visit the island.

After crossing the Granville Bridge, you'll ride on the busy surface streets through downtown. It's not as hard as it sounds, since traffic is slow and drivers have been trained by professional bike messengers to share the streets with bicyclists. The heart of this city is a surprisingly friendly place, alive with people and business. You'll take Nelson Street, which has relatively light traffic, back to Stanley Park and Lost Lagoon.

Mile for mile, few routes pack more experiences than this urban Vancouver ride.

The Basics

Start: Lost Lagoon, the southeast corner of Stanley Park, at Georgia and Chilco streets. If you don't have a bicycle, you can rent one there.

Length: 33 miles.

Terrain: There is a little of everything on this ride: separated paths, quiet neighborhood streets, and some busy suburban roads. It includes a ride through downtown Vancouver.

Food: Numerous stores and snack bars along the way. Whatever your taste, you'll find plenty to enjoy on this ride.

For more information: Bike Hotline, City of Vancouver, 453 W. 12th Ave., Vancouver, B.C.; (604) 871–6070. Bicycling Association of BC, 332 1367 W. Broadway, Vancouver, B.C. V6H 4A9; (604) 737–3034.

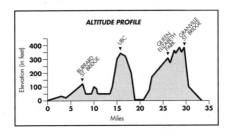

Miles & Directions

- 0.0 From Lost Lagoon, take the pedestrian tunnel under Georgia St. You now have a choice: Either follow the well-marked

Seawall bike path to the right, or ride on Stanley Park Dr., which follows closely inland. The Seawall path is often crowded and includes short stretches where cyclists are required to walk. Fast riders prefer Stanley Park Dr. Either way bicyclists must travel in a counterclockwise direction to minimize congestion on these popular routes.

- 5.7 Exit Stanley Park. Continue on Beach Ave.
- 6.5 Continue straight on Pacific St.
- 7.0 Turn right onto the Burrard Bridge sidewalk.
- 7.5 Turn right on Chestnut St., the first right turn. Pass the MacMillan Planetarium and Centennial Museum on your right.
- 7.8 Turn left on Ogden Ave. The Maritime Museum will be on your right. You are now on the designated Seaside bike route. Follow the green signs through Kitsilano Beach Park to Trafalgar St.

- *8.8 For an easier ride on low-traffic streets, follow the designated bike route 1 block past Cornwall Ave., right on York, left on Stephens, and then right on 3rd Ave. When 3rd Ave. dead-ends into Wallace, turn right. (Faster riders will prefer to turn right on Cornwall Ave., which is more direct and offers better sea views. Cornwall Ave. becomes Pt. Grey Rd.)*

- 10.5 Pt. Grey Rd. and the 3rd Ave. bike route rejoin at the Jericho Beach parking lot. Follow the beach path or, for faster riding, Marine Dr.
- 13.0 Continue on NW Marine Dr. If you have been riding on the path, you must now merge onto the roadway. Pacific Spirit Park forest is on your left.
- 14.0 The University of British Columbia is on your left.

The next section includes a 1-mile stretch of unpaved paths. To avoid it simply continue on SW Marine Dr. until the left turn at 57th Ave., then follow instructions from mile 22.1.

- 18.0 Turn right on Kullahun (watch for the Shaughnessy Golf Course sign), then an immediate left onto Salish Dr. Follow Salish around a curve and down the hill.

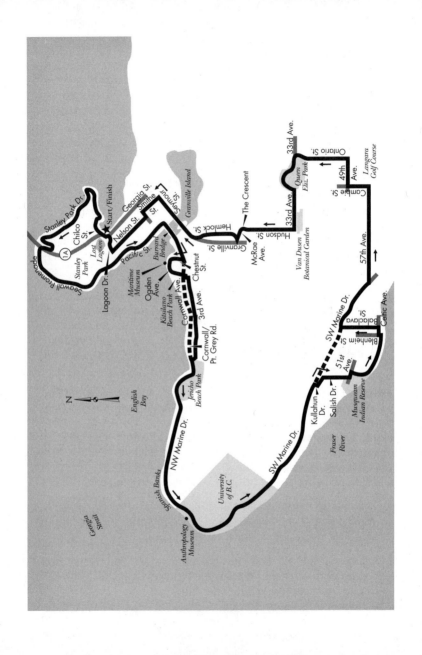

- 19.0 Turn left on 51st Ave.
- 19.2 Just past the Musqueam Golf Center, turn right onto the bridle path, which follows a small creek.
- 19.7 Turn left to follow the path along the Fraser River.
- 20.4 When the path ends at Blenheim St., turn left then immediately right onto Celtic Ave.
- 20.5 Turn left onto Balaclava St.
- 21.0 Turn right back onto Marine Dr.
- 22.1 Turn left onto 57th Ave.
- 24.0 When 57th deadends, turn left onto Cambie St.
- 24.5 Turn right onto 49th Ave.
- 25.0 Turn left onto Ontario St.
- 26.1 Left onto 33rd Ave. Take an immediate left into Queen Elizabeth Park, up a slight hill, and bear right at the first fork. Circle right around the park, past gardens and the lake.
- 27.0 Turn right onto 33rd Ave. going west.
- 27.8 Turn right onto Hudson St.
- 28.7 Turn right onto The Crescent, the street encircling a small round park. Ride three-quarters of the way around, and turn right onto McRae Ave. Where McRae dead-ends into 16th Ave., turn right, then take a quick left onto Hemlock St.
- 29.8 Follow Hemlock onto the Granville Bridge. Bicyclists are allowed to ride on the bridge roadway or you may walk on the sidewalk, with its excellent view of False Creek and beyond.
- 30.5 Bear right onto Seymour St. at the end of the bridge. In 5 blocks turn left onto Smithe St. After 5 more blocks turn left onto Thurlow St. In 2 blocks turn right onto Nelson St. You can now cross the heart of downtown Vancouver on this relatively low-traffic road.
- 32.6 You now enter the park. Turn right onto Lagoon Dr.
- 32.8 Turn left on Chilco, crossing the sidewalk (cars cannot enter). This puts you back at your starting point.
- 33.0 End.

5

Fort Langley Ramble

*Fort Langley—Langley
Telegraph Hill—Fort Langley*

Of the many excellent bicycle routes in the Fraser River Valley, this particular one is especially recommended by members of the Vancouver Bicycling Club. The route features scenic rural landscapes with great views of the Fraser River and nearby mountains. Parks and museums along the way offer glimpses into the area's colorful history, both human and natural. This is a good ride for children.

Fort Langley, our starting point, is considered the "Birthplace of British Columbia." The original fort was built by the Hudson's Bay Company in 1827 as a depot for furs and supplies. Soon a small farming community developed in the area. During the Fraser River gold rush of 1858, thousands of prospectors arrived, causing the British authorities to officially declare the region a colony. James Douglas was sworn in that year as the first British Columbia governor at Fort Langley, making it the province's first capital.

Rich with the history of both native and pioneer life, the Langley Centennial Museum and the Fort Langley National Historic Park are worthwhile to explore. Costumed staff demonstrate the skills of Canadian pioneers, from barrel making to blacksmithing. Kids and adults alike can learn history lessons through games and tastings of delicious foods cooked in old-fashioned ovens. For more information, call Fort Langley National Historic Park at (604) 888–4424.

The ride proceeds for 4 miles along the south shore of the

Fraser River, then turns inland on the old County Line Road, now called 264th Street. Follow this up a steep hill, then over rolling forested hills and across the Trans-Canada Highway. There you'll pass the Vancouver Game Farm, where, for a fee, you can see more than seventy species of animals from all over the world living in open pastures.

For a longer ride continue south on 264th, crossing the Fraser Highway. A series of moderately busy roads with shoulders will take you through an area of open pastureland and easy rolling hills. The Old Yale Road is a pleasant, low-traffic road that ends at the Fraser Highway, which you follow for about a mile. Although the highway carries heavy traffic, speeds are low and the shoulder is good as it becomes Main Street in the town of Langley. With a wide selection of restaurants, stores, and bakeries, Langley is an ideal lunch stop for hungry bicyclists. Turn right on Glover Road in downtown Langley, and that will take you back to Fort Langley.

The shorter ride follows pleasant, low-traffic roads through woods, farms, and residential areas. After crossing back over the Trans-Canada Highway, you'll ride on Telegraph Trail Road, which was part of the overland telegraph route established in 1865. You'll climb a hill, then descend the winding road to the lowland farms and wetlands along Rawlinson Creek Road. It's a short trip on Glover Road back to Fort Langley.

If you still have time for adventure, take the ferry to Maple Ridge, just north of Fort Langley and across the Fraser River, where you'll discover another popular bicycling area. Stop by the Fort Langley Tourist Information office on Mavis Street (just before the Fort Langley National Park) for information and locally produced maps of additional recommended cycling routes.

The Basics

Start: Fort Langley National Historic Park. Take the Fort Langley exit from the Trans-Canada Hwy., about 30 miles east of Vancouver. Go north about 7 miles, following signs to park.

Length: 22.7 or 32 miles.

Terrain: Mostly excellent low-traffic rural roads, rolling hills, and a 300-foot climb at 5 miles.

Food: Stores at 7.5 and 15 miles. Numerous stores and restaurants in Langley at 25 miles on the longer course.

For more information: Fort Langley Tourist Information Centre, P.O. Box 279, Fort Langley, B.C., V0X 1J0; (604) 888–1477.

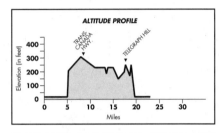

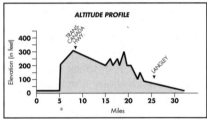

Miles & Directions

- 0.0 Turn right from the Fort Langley Park onto Mavis St., then an immediate right onto River Rd.
- 1.0 Take care crossing angled railroad tracks.
- 4.2 Turn right onto 264th St.
- 8.8 Cross over Trans-Canada Hwy., then pass the Vancouver Game Farm on the left.

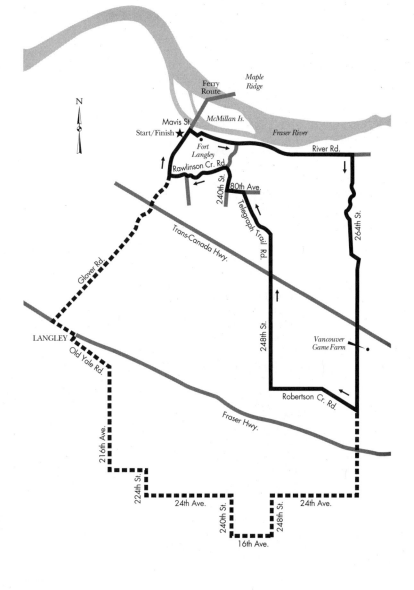

For shorter course—

- 11.0 Right onto Robertson Creek Rd.
- 13.0 Right onto 248th St. (Otter Rd.).
- 15.0 Village Market grocery store.
- 15.5 Cross back over Trans-Canada Hwy.
- 17.2 Begin Telegraph Trail Rd., a historic route established in 1865.
- 18.5 Turn left onto 80th Ave. (McKay Rd.).
- 18.3 Turn right onto 240th St.
- 18.8 Turn left onto Rawlinson Cr. Rd.
- 20.8 Bear right at 232nd to stay on Rawlinson Cr. Rd.
- 21.0 Turn right onto Glover Rd.
- 22.5 Turn right onto Mavis St.
- 22.7 End.

For longer course—

- 12.8 Turn right on 24th Ave.
- 14.8 Turn left on 248th St.
- 15.8 Turn right on 15th Ave.
- 16.8 Turn left on 240th St.
- 17.8 Turn left on 24th Ave.
- 19.8 Turn right on 224th St.
- 20.4 Turn left on 28th Ave.
- 21.4 Turn right on 216th (Johnston-Townline Rd.)
- 24.0 Bear left (a 45-degree turn) onto Old Yale Rd.
- 25.2 Where Old Yale ends turn left onto the Fraser Hwy., and follow it into downtown Langley.
- 26.0 Turn right onto Glover Rd.
- 32.0 End back at Fort Langley.

6

Harrison Hot Springs Challenge

Mission—Harrison Hot Springs—Agassiz Chilliwack—Mission

Randonneur bicyclists drink deeply where others merely sip. Randonneurs enjoy long-distance rides, with standard courses of 200, 300, 400, 600, and 1,000 kilometers. The 30 or 40 miles that many cyclists consider a good day's workout, randonneurs will ride before breakfast and be quickly off for more.

The Vancouver, British Columbia, area has an active Randonneur Club that sponsors regular training rides and events, including sanctioned rides that qualify participants for the famed Paris-Brest-Paris race. One of the group's favorite one-day rides is to cycle from Vancouver to Harrison Hot Springs on the north side of the Fraser River Valley, then return on the south side. It's an enjoyable route, especially the eastern section, where towering hills (they would be called mountains in other parts of the country) begin to constrict the valley.

The Harrison Hot Springs Challenge is a shorter version of this route, suitable for a fast one-day ride or a leisurely two-day trip with an overnight stop at the resort community of Harrison Hot Springs. Except for three mild climbs, this course stays on the flat valley floor.

The town of Mission, where the ride begins, is a friendly community spreading from the Fraser River up the south facing hillsides. The Fraser River Heritage Park is a worthwhile place to visit. Once the site of the original 1861 St. Mary's Mission, the park is now used for cultural and historical events during the spring, summer, and fall. Call park rangers at (604) 826–0277 for information on upcoming activities.

The first half of the ride follows the Lougheed Highway (Highway 7) through several small towns: Dewdney, Deroche, and Lake Errock. Don't blink or you'll miss them. You may want to stop along the way at Kilby Museum, a 1-mile round-trip detour, to experience an old-fashioned country store and a beautiful view from the bank of the Fraser River.

At Harrison Hot Springs you can soak those weary muscles in the hot pool or rest on the public beach of Harrison Lake. It's a tourist town with numerous opportunities for eating, shopping, and entertainment. Accommodations range from camping to first-class hotels and bed-and-breakfast facilities.

From Harrison ride south through Agassiz and across the Fraser River. The stretch of road from the bridge to the town of Chilliwack follows the river through quiet farmland. You'll ride a few miles of busy traffic through the towns of Chilliwack and Vedder Crossing, then more rural riding and a climb up Majuba Hill Road for a great view of the green valley.

The route passes through new suburban developments just outside Abbotsford, one of the growing commercial municipalities in the Fraser Valley. A series of rural farm roads leads back to the Fraser River, where you'll cross the towering Mission Bridge, which luckily has a separated pedestrian walkway, back to Mission.

The Basics

Start: N. Railway Ave. in downtown Mission. To get to Mission, exit the Trans-Canada Hwy. in Abbotsford, follow Hwy. 11 north, across the Fraser River.

Length: 86 miles.

Terrain: Mostly flat with a few hills and high bridges.

Food: Numerous stores and restaurants along the way.
For more information: Harrison Hot Springs Chamber of Commerce, P.O. Box 255, Harrison Hot Springs, B.C., V0M 1K0; (604) 796–3425.

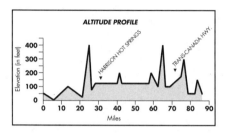

Miles & Directions

- 0.0 Head east on N. Railway Ave., which is the eastbound lane of the Lougheed Hwy. (Hwy. 7).
- 1.0 Merge onto highway.
- 5.0 Continue on highway through the town of Dewdney.
- 11.6 Pass through Deroche.
- 20.0 Turnoff to Kilby General Store Museum.
- 27.2 Left onto Cameron Rd.
- 28.2 Right onto McCallum Rd.
- 29.1 Left onto Hardy Rd.
- 30.0 Right onto Golf Rd.
- 30.5 Left onto Hot Springs Rd.
- 33.0 Harrison Hot Springs public baths to the right. Turn around.
- 36.7 Turn left onto Hwy. 7. Horn of Plenty Café at corner.
- 37.8 Bear right onto Hwy. 9. Follow the highway as it zigzags through Agassiz.
- 39.1 Curve right to continue on Hwy. 9, over the Fraser River bridge toward Chilliwack.
- 41.0 Just past the bridge make a left onto Rosedale Ferry Rd.

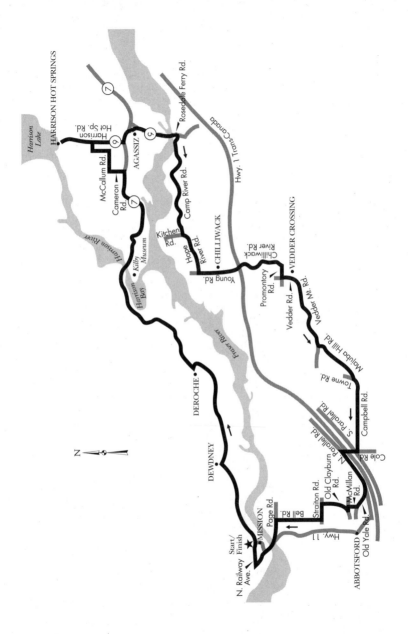

Follow the road under the bridge and through Ferry Island Provincial Park. Continue as this becomes Camp River Rd.

- 47.8 Turn left onto Kitchen Rd. at T intersection. Kitchen curves right to become Hope River Rd.
- 50.4 Turn left on Young Rd. Follow this through the town of Chilliwack.
- 52.9 Pass under Trans-Canada Hwy. 1.
- 53.0 Bear right onto Chilliwack River Rd.
- 56.5 Bear right onto Promontory Rd.
- 57.1 Left onto Vedder Rd.
- 58.2 Continue straight across the Chilliwack River. Follow the road as it curves right to become Vedder Mountain Rd.
- 62.3 Turn left on Majuba Hill Rd.
- 65.6 Turn left onto Towne Rd.
- 66.0 Follow the road as it curves right to become Campbell Rd.
- 70.0 Turn right at T onto Cole Rd.
- 70.7 Turn left onto S. Parallel Rd.
- 73.1 Turn right to cross bridge over Hwy. 1, then turn left onto N. Parallel Rd.
- 74.0 Bear left onto Old Yale Rd.
- 75.5 Right onto McMillan Rd.
- 76.4 Left onto High Dr., then at the bottom of a short incline turn right onto Old Clayburn Rd.
- 78.3 Left onto Straiton Rd.
- 79.2 Right onto Bell Rd.
- 82.0 Left onto Page Rd.
- 83.1 Left onto Riverside Rd.
- 83.3 Right onto Mission Bridge. Use pedestrian walkway.
- 84.2 Bear left toward Hwy. 7 west.
- 85.0 Turn right onto Hwy. 7.
- 86.0 End back at Mission.

Idaho

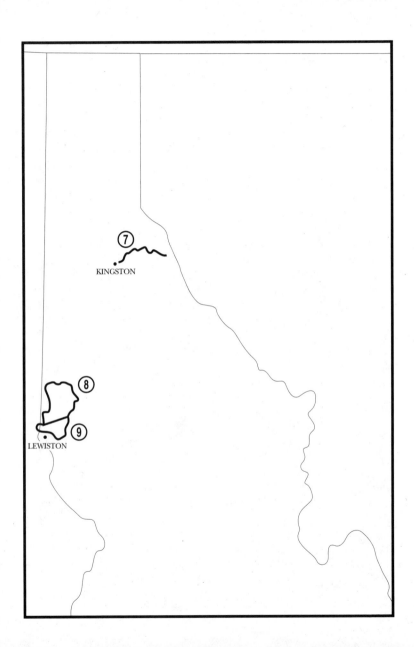

Idaho

7

Murray Cruise

Enaville—Murray—Prichard—Enaville

Much of the energy and enthusiasm in the Spokane Bicycle Club comes from a group of hard-riding women who call themselves the "Golden Girls." Most Tuesdays and Thursdays for the past twenty years, they have enjoyed a combination of bicycling and socializing, and they always extend a welcome to newcomers. Tuesdays are for easy rides of 10 to 25 miles. On Thursdays they often take longer rides that explore the byways and small communities outside the Spokane Valley. Despite their ages (ranging from late forties to midseventies), these women can leave behind many younger riders. Between them they have extensive touring experience, a lot of road "smarts," and the ability to squeeze a full serving of fun out of their bicycling adventures.

This route along the Coeur d'Alene River and up into Murray in northern Idaho is typical of these pleasant Thursday rides. The route begins at the Snake Pit, an old restaurant and tavern in Enaville. Soon you'll have the roads along the Coeur d'Alene River to yourself for relaxed bicycling.

It's an easy, steady grade through a beautiful river valley. Steep basalt cliffs and towering forest-covered hills above the crystal-clear river provide spectacular visual drama. During the spring you will see splashes of colorful wildflowers. Summer lends the heady smells of forests on a hot day. Autumn brings out the bright orange and yellow foliage of the tamarack trees sprinkled among the evergreens.

This region has experienced booms and busts. Huge piles of

mine tailings scattered along the road to Murray hint of bygone days when Murray was a miner's heaven. The town is now home to a few ranchers and is a popular destination for tourists. Bicyclists enjoy stopping there for lunch at the Sprag Pole Inn, which includes a wondrous museum of historical artifacts and curios. It's a fun place to browse. After a meal and a rest you'll be ready for the slightly easier ride back.

The Basics

Start: Ride starts at the Snake Pit in Enaville, Idaho. Go east on I–90 from Coeur d'Alene. Take the Kingston exit (no. 43), turn left over the freeway, and go 1.5 miles north.

Length: 58 miles.

Terrain: An easy river grade, light traffic.

Food: Babin's Grocery at 21 and 39 miles; store and restaurant in Murray, at 29 miles.

For more information: Coeur d'Alene Area Visitors Bureau, Box 1088N, Coeur d'Alene, ID 83814; (800) CDA–4YOU, (800) 544–9855 in Canada, (206) 664–0587 in Idaho.

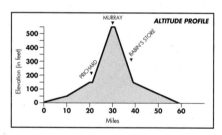

Miles & Directions

- 0.0 Turn right (north) from Snake Pit.
- 0.5 Turn right just before Henery's General Store. Follow road as it curves left onto the bridge over the Coeur d'Alene River,

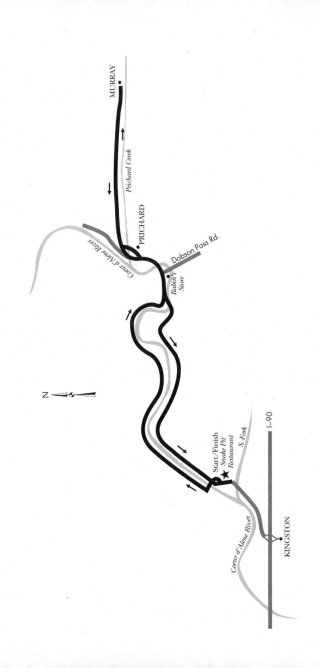

then turn right to follow the northwest riverbank. This is the Old Coeur d'Alene River Rd.

- 21.0 Babin's Grocery. Bear left at fork toward Prichard and Murray.
- 23.0 Turn right toward Prichard (the town consists of a tavern and a phone booth), cross Prichard Creek, then turn right to follow the creek toward Murray.
- 29.0 Turn around in Murray.
- 36.0 Turn left on highway.
- 37.5 Bear right at Babin's Grocery.
- 39.5 Bear left to cross river, follow road on the south side of river. This is the New Coeur d'Alene River Road.
- 58.0 End back at Enaville.

8

Twin River Classic

Hells Gate Park—Lapwai—Kendrick
Moscow—Lewiston

Early each autumn a small band of stalwart riders and their sup-
porters gather at Hells Gate State Park near Lewiston, Idaho, for
one of the most challenging rides included in this book: the Twin
River Cyclists Centennial Century Ride. It's an enjoyable trip for
bicyclists who are in shape for 100 miles of riding over the hilly
northern Idaho countryside. Other participants choose the easier
50- and 25-mile options described in the next ride.

It's cold at the beginning. Fortunately the route begins with a
mild warmup climb through the narrow Tammany Creek valley.
This is cowboy country, rich with the smell of hay and horses.
The grassland is dry and brown by this time of year, except in the
valleys where trees cluster around the narrow creek. Observant
riders will see plenty of wildlife along the way: hawks flying over-
head, quail among tumbleweeds, and deer grazing in the distance.

Eight miles out riders pass the Lewiston Roundup Rodeo arena.
A little farther, the valley opens into rolling hills, a pleasant
stretch of riding. By now everybody is warmed up, so you may be
surprised when the local riders stop to put their windbreakers back
on at the summit of a small hill. This is the top of the Webb
Grade, a long and steep descent most of the way to Lapwai, a
town on the Nez Percé Indian Reservation.

A few miles past Lapwai is the Nez Percé National Historical
Park, which includes a museum and park at the site of the Spalding Mission, adjacent to the Clearwater River. The route goes

through the park's picnic area, past a narrow gate, and onto the old highway, now closed to through motor vehicle traffic. Bicyclists usually have this whole side of the river to themselves for several pleasant miles of riding.

Crossing the Clearwater River, the route continues up the Potlatch River on Highway 3, a moderately hilly ride, through the town of Juliaetta to Kendrick. The 5-mile, 1,500-foot ascent out of Kendrick up Brady Gulch is the most challenging stretch of this route. It's pleasant for strong riders, a curving road through the dry pine forest that fills the narrow gulch up to the open grain fields that cover the hilly plateau. At the summit riders enjoy a spectacular view of the Palouse Hills.

It's 10 miles of rolling hills toward Troy. The route detours past the town, turning onto Highway 8 to Moscow, home of the University of Idaho. It passes through an industrial section, which doesn't do justice to this pleasant community. Following Highway 95 south riders must climb some last steep hills going out of town.

From Moscow it's a relatively straight shot south to the top of the Old Lewiston Grade, a narrow winding road built early in the century, appropriately called the "Spiral Highway." From the top riders enjoy an excellent view of the confluence of the Snake and Clearwater rivers, with Lewiston to the left, Clarkston to the right, and Hells Gate Canyon to the south. Right below, curving back and forth down the hill, the Spiral Highway descends 1,800 feet down to the river valley.

Check your brakes before starting. It's an enjoyable ride down if you like windy roads. The narrow highway, fortunately well banked, has twenty hairpin turns, which demand constant attention. The traffic is usually light (most vehicles use the new, wider highway).

Crossing the Clearwater River into Lewiston, you can join the extensive trail system along the river levees going all the way back to Hells Gate Park. There are historical displays along the trails and plenty of places to stop for a rest. Some local riders prefer to ride through downtown Lewiston on surface streets, but this can be difficult for bicyclists unfamiliar with the town and the hazardous angled railroad crossings on Snake River Avenue.

Hells Gate Park is an enjoyable site, but never more so than after a hundred miles of challenging bicycling. Cyclists who finish the Twin River Classic can feel mighty proud for having completed one of the most difficult rides in the Northwest.

The Basics

Start: Hells Gate State Park, 4 miles south of Lewiston. Turn south on Snake River Ave. from Hwy. 12, just east of the Snake River bridge.

Length: 101.5 miles.

Terrain: Some steady river grades, lots of rolling hills, and a few major climbs, including a 1,500-foot ascent up Brady Gulch. Roads are generally good.

Food: Stores and restaurants in Lapwai, at 20 miles; in Juliaetta, at 35.8 miles; Kendrick, at 39.8 miles; Moscow, at 61.4; and Lewiston, at 95.1. Take plenty of water.

For more information: Twin River Bicycling Club, c/o River City Schwinn, Lewiston Center, Lewiston, ID 83501; (208) 746–0961.

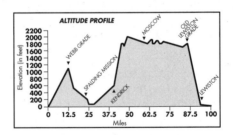

Miles & Directions

- 0.0 Exit park, turn right onto Tammany Creek Rd. (Hwy. 505).
- 7.4 Turn right, to stay on Tammany Rd. (Hwy. 505). Pass Tammany School and Lewiston Roundup rodeo arenas.
- 11.5 Bear left at Y; continue on Hwy. 505.

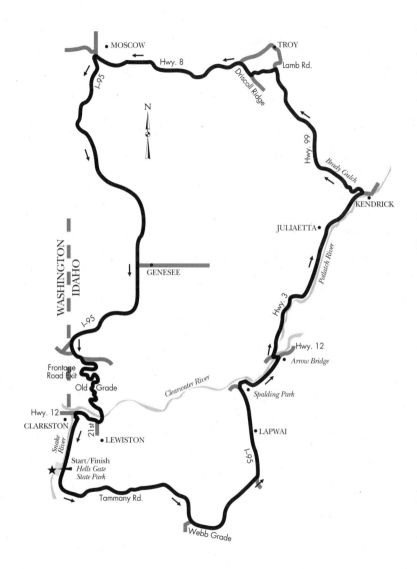

MOSCOW

TROY

Hwy. 8

Lamb Rd.

Driscoll Ridge

I-95

N

Hwy. 99

Brady Gulch

KENDRICK

JULIAETTA

Potlatch River

WASHINGTON
IDAHO

GENESEE

Hwy. 3

I-95

Hwy. 12

Arrow Bridge

Frontage
Road Exit

Clearwater River

Old Grade

Spalding Park

Hwy. 12

CLARKSTON

21st

LEWISTON

LAPWAI

Snake
River

Start/Finish
Hells Gate
State Park

I-95

Tammany Rd.

Webb Grade

- 17.4 Turn left onto I–95, north to Lapwai.
- 20.0 Lapwai. Trading Post and café.
- 24.0 Turn right into Spalding Mission National Historical Park. Follow road past the visitor center and down a small hill to the mission site. Turn left at T, then curve right to cross small bridge, past the cemetery and picnic area. Pass through gate to the old highway along the Clearwater River.
- 27.3 Turn left onto Hwy. 12, across the Clearwater River. At the opposite side of the bridge turn right on Hwy. 3 to follow the Potlatch River north.
- 36.0 Juliaetta.
- 40.0 Turn left in Kendrick onto Hwy. 99, toward Troy. For the next 5 miles you will be climbing Brady Gulch.
- 45.0 Summit!
- 50.3 Turn left onto Lamb Rd. Follow road as it curves and becomes Driscoll Ridge.
- 52.9 Bear left at Y.
- 53.4 Turn left onto Hwy. 8, going west.
- 61.4 Turn left onto Hwy. 95 in Moscow.
- 84.6 Bear left to stay on Hwy. 95.
- 86.2 Turn right onto the Old Lewiston Grade. Check your brakes in preparation for an exciting, curvy descent.
- 93.5 Turn left onto Down River Rd.
- 94.4 Merge right onto Hwy. 12, toward Lewiston. Cross the Clearwater River, and follow the roadway as it curves right across the bridge.
- 95.2 Make an acute right just past Locomotive Park, then left at Engine no. 92 down the alley toward the river, and cross two sets of railroad tracks. Turn left on the levee trail, and follow it back to Hells Gate State Park.
- 101.5 End.

9

Lewiston Cruise

Hells Gate Park—Lapwai—Lewiston

The shorter options of the Twin River Cyclists annual Centennial Ride are extremely enjoyable routes through the dry country north of the Snake River. Like the more difficult Twin River Classic, they start out following Tammany Creek up to the Lewiston Roundup arena. The 25-mile course turns to climb a small hill and then descends Lindsay Creek Road through the narrow canyon into the town of Lewiston. Riders can then either cross the Clearwater River to Clarkston or take the shorter, easier ride along recreational paths back to the park.

The 50-mile course continues up to the Webb Grade, where riders enjoy a fast descent down to Lapwai, a community on the Nez Percé Indian Reservation. You can stop at the Trading Post to buy food for a picnic or eat at the café. A few miles past Lapwai, the route turns off Interstate 95 at the Spalding Mission National Historical Park. The interpretive center has fascinating displays well worth a visit, and bicyclists can rest under cool trees along the river. It's an ideal picnic site. Past the park the route follows the old highway, now closed to through traffic, for a delightful ride along the Clearwater River.

Crossing the Clearwater, the route follows Highway 12. This highway has heavy truck traffic carrying timber, wood chips, and grain, but a wide shoulder makes riding easy. The route continues west, crossing the Clearwater River into Clarkston on the Washington side of the border. Looping back under the bridge and along the city's industrial waterfront, the route crosses back to

Lewiston and follows the delightful bike path along the Snake River levee back to Hells Gate Park.

The Basics

Start: Hells Gate State Park, 4 miles south of Lewiston. Turn south on Snake River Ave. from Hwy. 12, just east of the Snake River bridge.
Length: 50.4 or 25.4 miles.
Terrain: Relatively easy river grades and rolling hills. The 50-mile option includes the Webb Grade, a steep 600-foot descent.
Food: Stores and restaurants in Lapwai, at 20 miles; in Juliaetta, at 35.8 miles; Clarkston, at 45 miles. Take plenty of water.
For more information: Lewiston Chamber of Commerce, 2207 E. Main, Lewiston, ID, 83501; (208) 743–3531.

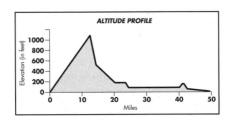

Miles & Directions

- 0.0 Exiting the park, turn right on Tammany Rd. (Hwy. 505).
- 7.4 Turn right to stay on Tammany Rd. (Hwy. 505). Pass the Tammany School and rodeo arenas.

For 25-mile option—

- 8.0 Turn left onto 21st St., opposite the rodeo-arena parking entrance.
- 9.1 Turn right on Grelle Ave., then an immediate left onto Lindsay Creek Rd.

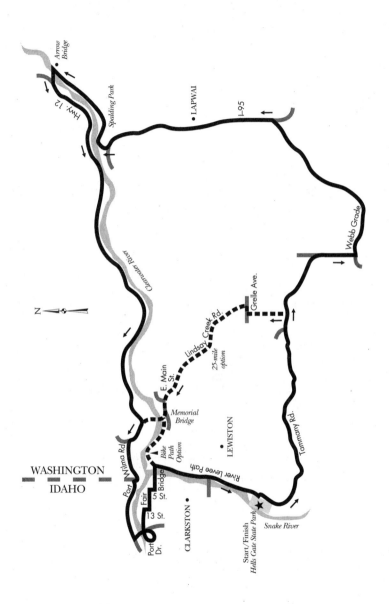

- 13.5 Turn left at stop sign onto Main St., going west.
- 14.2 Turn right onto bridge to cross the Clearwater River. (For a shorter, easier ride, continue on Main St., make an acute right after Locomotive Park, and turn left at Engine no. 93, down the alley toward the river. Turn left on the levee trail, and take it back to Hells Gate Park.)
- 16.0 Turn left at the second light onto Down River Rd. Continue following instructions below at mile 40.1.

For 50-mile option—

- 11.5 Bear left at Y, continue on Hwy. 505.
- 12.6 Top of Webb Grade. Prepare for fast descent.
- 17.4 Turn left onto I–95, north to Lapwai.
- 20.0 Lapwai. Trading Post and café.
- 24.0 Turn right, into the Spalding Mission National Historical Park. Follow the road past the visitor's center, down to the mission site. Turn left at T, then curve right to cross small bridge. Continue past cemetery and picnic area. Pass through gate to follow the old highway along the Clearwater River.
- 27.3 Turn left onto Hwy. 12, and cross the Clearwater River. Across the bridge turn left to stay on Hwy. 12, going toward Lewiston along the Clearwater River.
- 39.4 Bear left at fork to continue on Hwy. 12.
- 40.1 Bear right onto Hwy. 128, toward the port districts.
- 44.0 Turn left to cross bridge to Clarkston. At the opposite side of the bridge, take the first right, which curves back, past marina, under the bridge.
- 45.6 After the road curves to the right, turn left onto Fair St. After stop sign bear right onto 2nd St., then turn left at Bridge St., taking the bridge sidewalk. Across the river take the stairs down to the levee trail. Ride the trail back to Hells Gate Park.
- 50.4 End.

Oregon

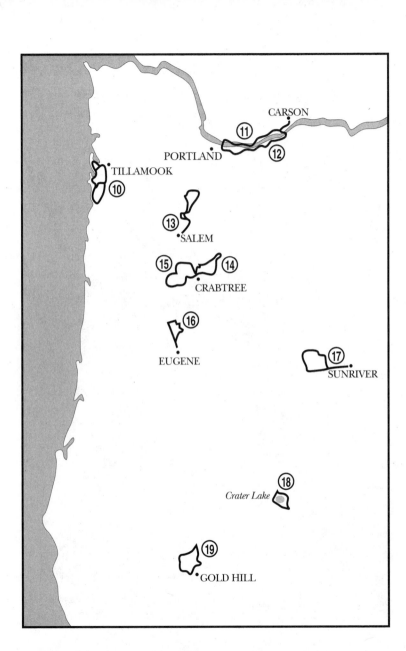

Oregon

10

Three Capes Scenic Cruise

Tillamook—Cape Meares—Netarts
Cape Lookout—Pleasant Valley—Tillamook

Every year thousands of cyclists from all over the world enjoy the splendor and challenge of riding the Oregon coastline. It's a rugged and beautiful area of spray-covered cliffs, sandy beaches scattered with driftwood logs, and brilliant evergreen forests. The Oregon coast is so popular with bicyclists that the Oregon Department of Transportation has designated an official bicycle route. Communities along the way, accustomed to cyclists, tend to be bicycle-friendly, and the numerous state parks reserve special campsites to accommodate bicyclists.

The Three Capes Scenic Cruise is a one-day option for cyclists who wish to enjoy the best of the Oregon Coast Bicycle Route without devoting a week or more to the ride. The Three Capes route offers something for all tastes: local history, extraordinary views, and opportunities to enjoy the seafood and dairy products for which this region is famous.

The ride begins in the town of Tillamook, at the Pioneer Museum, a repository of local historic paraphernalia, old photographs, and lifelike natural history displays. There you can learn about the region's traditional industries, including logging, fishing, and dairy farming, and get a feel for pioneer life, when small ships provided the only transport between small communities scattered along the coast.

Riding from Tillamook past delta-land dairy farms, you'll follow the south shore of Tillamook Bay. Bay Ocean Spit, which forms the bay, is a wildlife sanctuary supporting more than two hundred species of birds. Developers once planned a huge urban metropolis called Ocean City at the Spit's south end, but the steady action of wind and waves slowly washed away the town, returning the coastline to its pristine state. A few miles farther you'll climb the cliffs to enjoy dramatic views; below you'll see giant breakers crashing against towering offshore rocks and sand beaches, all framed in wind-sculpted trees. At the summit you can enjoy an even better view at the Cape Meares lighthouse (built in 1890). Here old-growth spruce and hemlock forests give way to vertical sea cliffs where tufted puffins, cormorants, and pigeon guillemots nest.

Farther down the coast you can take a short detour at the community of Oceanside to see Three Arch Rocks National Wildlife Refuge, Oregon's largest seabird nesting site. With the help of field glasses, you can view some of the more than seventy-five thousand common murres that nest there. You can also satisfy your appetite in Oceanside at Rosanna's Restaurant, or buy a picnic lunch at one of the stores in Netarts.

The route divides at Netarts Bay. The 21-mile option curves directly back to Tillamook. The two longer routes offer steep climbs, welcome descents, bay-side riding, and more magnificent views of the rugged coastline. After riding south along the shore, the return trip on Highway 101 seems tame and pastoral. Passing miles of green pastures and munching cows, you'll see why Tillamook County is famous for its dairy herds and cheese production.

After returning to the Pioneer Museum, you may want to take the 2-mile ride north to the cooperatively owned Tillamook Cheese Factory for a walk-through tour, which ends with a wide selection of tasty snacks. However you ride it you'll find this route a multi-sensory delight!

The Basics

Start: Pioneer Museum, 1st St. (Hwy. 6) and Pacific Ave. (Hwy. 101) in Tillamook.

Length: 21, 41.7, or 64 miles.

Terrain: Mostly flat with a few big hills.

Food: Rosanna's Restaurant at 12 miles; stores in Netarts, at 13.8 miles; Wee Willie's Restaurant at 17 miles; and South Prairie Store at 37.6 miles (41.7-mile route). Stores in Pacific City, Hebo, and Beaver on the 64-mile route.

For more information: Coast Bicycle Route maps available from Bicycle Program Manager, Oregon Department of Transportation, Room 200, Transportation Building, Salem, OR 97310; (503) 378–3432.

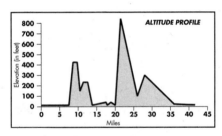

Miles & Directions

- 0.0 Leaving the museum, take 2nd Ave. 3 blocks west, turn left on Stillwell, then right onto 3rd Ave., which becomes the Netarts Hwy.
- 2.0 After crossing the Tillamook River, turn right onto Bay Ocean Rd. This road follows the south shore of Tillamook Bay.
- 3.3 Momaloose County Park boat ramp, public rest rooms.
- 7.0 Ocean Bay Spit. The dirt road goes out to Kincheloe Point, a popular bird-watching site.
- 7.3 Turn left, following the Oregon Coast Bicycle Route sign.
- 9.4 Cape Meares State Park. Facilities and lighthouse are a .5-mile ride (and 200-foot descent) into the park.

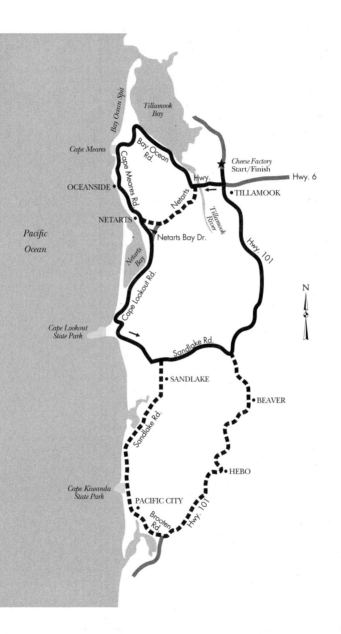

- 12.0 Turn left, following the Oregon Coast Bicycle Route sign. To the right is Oceanside, Three Arch Rocks, and Rosanna's Restaurant.
- 13.8 Netarts.
- 14.4 Turn right on Netarts Bay Dr.

For 21-mile option, bear left. Continue on Netarts Bay Dr. as it curves back to Tillamook.

- 16.0 Bear right onto Whisky Creek/Cape Lookout Rd.
- 19.8 Pass Cape Lookout State Park entrance.
- 22.5 Wildlife-viewing area.
- 26.0 Continue straight toward Hwy. 101 on Sandlake Rd.

For a 64-mile ride, turn right toward Sandlake and Pacific City. From Pacific City, follow Brooten Rd. toward Hwy. 101. Turn left on Hwy. 101 and follow it back to Tillamook.

- 30.3 Turn left on Hwy. 101 to Tillamook.
- 36.7 Rest area to left.
- 41.0 Enter Tillamook. Hwy. 101 becomes Pacific Ave. through town.
- 41.7 Turn right at 2nd St., and end back at Pioneer Museum.

11

Carson Hot Springs Challenge

Portland—Camas—Beacon Rock
Bonneville Dam—Stevenson—Carson

This pair of bicycle rides nourishes both the body and the soul. The Carson Hot Springs Challenge takes you along the Washington side of the Columbia River Gorge to Carson Hot Springs. There you can pamper your body with a soak in the healthful mineral waters, a professional massage, and a relaxed stay at this charming resort. The companion ride, the Carson Return Challenge, takes you along the Oregon side of the river back to your starting point. The combination of hard riding, spectacular scenery, and pampering has long made Carson Hot Springs a popular destination with Portland area bicyclists.

This ride begins in northeast Portland, where you take advantage of the bike path down the center of the Glen Jackson bridge. This path offers bicyclists a unique experience, as you ride safely for 2.5 miles between lanes of high-speed motor vehicle traffic 200 feet above the Columbia River and Government Island game refuge. Once you climb to the bridge's summit, it's an easy coast to the city of Vancouver on the Washington side, where you catch the old Evergreen Highway. Although narrow and in need of maintenance, this road has relatively light traffic, making it the preferred route for bicycling.

The Evergreen Highway will take you 10 miles east along the

bank of the Columbia River through the towns of Camas and Washougal. From there the route follows Highway 14 along one of the most beautiful and dramatic stretches of the Columbia River Gorge. Be sure to fill your water bottles, because a few miles out of Washougal you'll face the most difficult climb of this trip, a 900-foot ascent called Cape Horn. It's a rewarding challenge: As you get higher the views become better and better, with the river below, towering cliffs on the Oregon side, and the cone of Mount Hood floating in the distance.

It's an easy descent to Skamania, a one-store community. A few miles farther you will pass Beacon Rock State Park. This 848-foot natural tower was the basalt core, or "throat," of a volcano. It was appropriately named: When travelers down the Columbia River saw Beacon Rock, they knew that the difficult rapids were passed and no further obstructions remained to the Pacific Ocean. If Cape Horn isn't enough climbing in one day, hike the trail to the top of Beacon Rock.

Beyond Beacon Rock you will pass the town of North Bonneville. This is a new community, built to replace the original town, which was flooded when the Bonneville Dam was raised to a higher level in 1976. The town features an extensive bike and pedestrian pathway system, and 2 miles east of the town, you can explore the Bonneville Dam. The visitor center there offers tours of enormous generators and fish ladders, as well as displays on the history of this power source.

At mile 46 you'll turn off Highway 14, climb 1 mile to the town of Carson, then down to the welcome site of the Carson Hot Mineral Springs Resort along the Wind River. The resort has long been a popular destination for people seeking rest and cures for ailments ranging from rheumatism to stomach disorders. The mineral springs were first discovered in 1876, and the St. Martins Hotel was built in 1897. The mineral water, which is pumped from farther up the river, is a natural 126 degrees. The baths themselves are giant old claw-foot tubs, which are filled to your preferred temperature. After you have been soaking for half an hour, a uniformed attendant will wrap you in sheets and let you lie quietly on a cot in total relaxation. A cooling shower completes the treatment. You can also make an appointment for a professional massage. It is an ideal way to end a day of hard bicycling.

The resort is busy, especially during weekends, so make reservations well in advance, both for your room and your bath or massage. Prices are surprisingly low for bath treatments, rooms, and cabins. The resort also includes a charming restaurant and miles of trails through beautiful forests. People who prefer to soak out in the open can hike the 1.5-mile trail to natural hot-spring pools in the woods beside the Wind River.

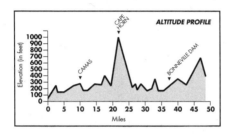

The Basics

Start: The bike path at the south end of the I–205, Glen Jackson Bridge, in northeast Portland. By car, exit I–205 at NE Airport Way or at Columbia Blvd. You can park in the airport parking lot, then take Airport Way east .5 mile, turn left on NE 122nd Ave., then left on NE Marine Dr., and enter the trail system where Marine Dr. passes under the I–205 bridge. You can also park on residential streets in the Parkrose area, then follow the bike path north from Columbia Blvd. near the intersection with Sandy Blvd.

Length: 48.2 miles.

Terrain: Bike path across the Columbia River bridge, old road with light traffic along the Evergreen Hwy. to Camas, moderately busy highway with good shoulders the rest of the way to Carson; one 900-foot climb.

Food: There are stores and restaurants in Camas, at 10 miles; Washougal, at 12 miles; and Stevenson, at 42.6 miles. There is a

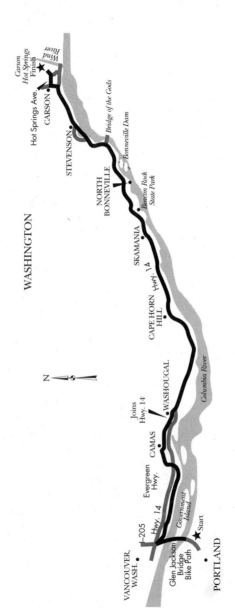

store in Skamania, at 30.7 miles; café in Carson, at 46.8 miles; and restaurant at Carson Hot Springs, at 47.8 miles.

For more information: Carson Hot Mineral Springs, P.O. Box 370, Carson, WA 98610; (509) 427–8292. Skamania County Chamber of Commerce, P.O. Box 1037, Stevenson, WA 98648; (509) 427–8911.

Miles & Directions

- 0.0 Take the bike path on the Glen Jackson Bridge over the Columbia River.
- 2.5 On the north side of the bridge, follow the path as it curves left and ends on 23rd St. in Vancouver, Washington. Head west on 23rd St., and turn left when it deadends on Ellsworth.
- 3.0 Turn left onto SE Evergreen Hwy., an old highway designated as a bike route, which follows the Columbia River shore.
- 6.0 Continue straight at stop sign in front of cemetery.
- 10.0 Follow the road as it curves over Hwy. 14 entering Camas. Turn right at stop sign onto NW 6th Ave.
- 11.0 Follow the arterial as it turns right onto Adams and then left onto 3rd Ave., through downtown Camas. Continue through the town of Washougal.
- 16.6 Turn right, then left onto Hwy. 14 going east.
- 21.7 Cape Horn Climb.
- 30.7 Skamania store.
- 32.6 Beacon Rock State Park.
- 37.6 Bonneville Dam visitor center.
- 42.6 Stevenson.
- 45.8 Turn left on Wind River Rd. toward the town of Carson.
- 46.8 Turn right on Hot Springs Ave. in Carson.
- 47.8 Turn left on St. Martins Springs Rd., and descend into the Carson Hot Mineral Springs Resort.
- 48.2 End at St. Martins Hotel.

12

Carson Hot Springs
Return Challenge

*Carson Hot Springs—Multnomah Falls
Crown Point—Troutdale—Portland*

This is the return trip of the Carson Hot Springs Challenge. It is a
spectacular ride, following the Historic Columbia River Scenic
Highway through the Columbia River Gorge National Scenic Area,
with many delightful and impressive sights along the way. The
Scenic Highway is used for many organized bicycle rides, including the Portland Wheelmen Touring Club's Gorge Challenge Century. This ride is accurately described as a Challenge; the Scenic
Highway is a narrow road that winds along the gorge and often
carries heavy tourist traffic.

Starting from Carson Hot Mineral Springs Resort, you will ride
Highway 14 back to Stevenson. There you may want to explore
the Skamania County Historical Museum and enjoy the friendly
ambience of this riverfront town. Just south of town you can turn
off Highway 14 and ride on the quiet side of Rock Cove. Rock
Cove Park, an enjoyable place to rest or picnic, has displays of antique logging equipment.

Continue on Highway 14 until you cross the Columbia River
on the "Bridge of the Gods." This narrow toll bridge stands at the
site of the Cascade Rapids, now buried beneath the Bonneville
Dam reservoir. Native American mythology describes a land
bridge built by the gods at this site that they used to cross the

river. Geologists believe that landslides may have created a temporary crossing many years ago, giving the myth a historical basis. Whatever the origins of its impressive name, the bridge offers a breathtaking ride over its metal-grid surface. Look down to the river below—if you don't fear heights—and ride with care.

After paying a 25-cent toll, you circle down onto the main highway. You'll then ride for 6 miles on the shoulder of I–84. Take a break from the freeway by stopping at the Bonneville Dam, at mile 13.4, where you can see ships moving through the navigation lock and learn about salmon migration and power generation. Turning off and crossing under the freeway at 16.5 miles, you'll begin to ride on the less-traveled Scenic Historic Columbia River Highway.

Built under the direction of engineer Samual Lancaster between 1913 and 1922, this highway is a registered National Historic Civil Engineering Landmark. It is lined with fantastic waterfalls, several state parks, the Columbia River, and intricate stonework lookouts and guardrails. While riding you may notice differences between the two sides of the gorge: The steep, green cliffs of the south bank of the Columbia are wetter and cooler than the gentle, sunbaked slopes to the north. Along the Scenic Highway you will pass Horsetail, Wahkeena, Bridal Veil, Shepperd's Dell, and Latourell falls—any of which deserve a visit. This lush and moist environment contrasts sharply with the drier hills you climbed while riding on the Washington side.

At mile 23 you'll probably want to stop at Multnomah Falls, alongside the highway. This magnificent 620-foot cascade is one of the highest year-round waterfalls in the United States and certainly one of the most beautiful. You can enjoy a fine lunch in the elegant Multnomah Falls Lodge, visit the National Forest Service's Nature Interpretive Center, and, if you have extra energy, hike to the top of the falls.

After lunch at Multnomah Falls, you'll have a few easy miles of riding before beginning the arduous climb up to Vista House (built in 1917) at Crown Point. Give yourself plenty of rests while climbing, and, out of courtesy to drivers, pull off the narrow highway if you delay other vehicles. At the summit on a clear day, you can enjoy a reward for your efforts: a 30-mile view of the gorge.

It's an easy descent toward Portland through farmland and woods and through the small community of Corbett. At the end of the descent, you pass beautiful Dabney State Park, where pleasant shade trees hang over the Sandy River. Follow this river down to Troutdale, where you join a separated path parallel to Marine Drive along the Columbia River. This is part of the popular 40 Mile Loop, a regional trail system designed to connect more than thirty parks in the Portland area. Some stretches of this path follow right along the Columbia River shore, offering views of houseboats, river traffic, and forested islands. The many joyful bicyclists and pedestrians who share the trails will offer you a festive welcome back to your starting point in Portland.

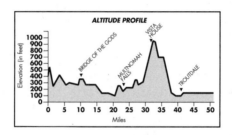

The Basics

Start: Carson Hot Springs Resort in Carson, Washington. This is the return trip for the Carson Hot Springs Challenge.

Length: 51 miles.

Terrain: Most of this route follows older scenic highways. Some stretches are in good shape. Other stretches are narrow, poorly maintained, and adjacent to cliffs. The ride includes a 700-foot climb. Traffic can be heavy during the summer tourist season.

Food: Stores and restaurants in Stevenson, at 6.5 miles; and Troutdale, at 41 miles. Multnomah Falls Lodge is at 23 miles, and there are grocery stores at 34 and 37 miles.

For more information: Portland Area 40 Mile Loop Land Trust,

Portland Parks Dept., 23rd Floor, 900 SW 5th Ave., Portland, OR 97204; (503) 823–2223 (maps available for a small fee).

Miles & Directions

- 0.0 Ride up St. Martins Rd., and turn left onto Hot Springs Ave. at the top.
- 1.4 Turn right onto Hwy. 14.
- 6.5 Town of Stevenson.

    For a short but pleasant alternative route around Rock Cove, turn right onto the Second Street Ext. at the west end of town, past Rock Creek Park and Fairgrounds.

- 8.0 Alternative route turns right back onto Hwy. 14.
- 9.5 Turn left onto the Bridge of the Gods. Ride carefully over this metal-grid surface. On the Oregon side pay a 25-cent toll, then circle down toward the river, and turn left (west) onto Hwy. 30.
- 10.7 Take ramp onto Hwy. 84. Ride on the shoulder of this limited-access highway.
- 13.4 Pass Bonneville Dam visitor information center.
- 16.5 Exit I–84. At the bottom of the off-ramp, turn left, go under the freeway, then turn right on the old highway toward Portland.
- 18.8 Turn left at stop sign to follow the Historic Columbia River Scenic Hwy. toward Portland and Multnomah Falls.
- 20.5 Horsetail Falls.
- 23.0 Multnomah Falls and Restaurant.
- 26.0 Turn left at fork to stay on the Historic Scenic Hwy.
- 27.0 Turnoff to Bridal Veil State Park.
- 31.4 Crown Point State Park, Vista House.
- 34.0 Corbett Country Market.
- 35.3 Bear left at fork to stay on Scenic Hwy.
- 37.0 Bear left after market to stay on Scenic Hwy.
- 38.0 Pass Dabney State Park, on the banks of Sandy River.

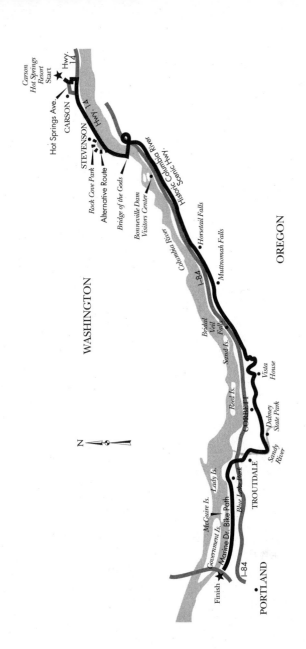

- 41.0 Turn left to cross bridge over Sandy River. Follow road as it curves right then left through downtown Troutdale.
- 42.0 Turn right on 257th Dr., part of Portland's 40 Mile Loop. Turn left after passing under I–84, following Bike Route signs toward Marine Dr.
- 42.6 Bear right onto Marine Dr. In about a mile a separated path parallels the roadway. Continue on 40 Mile Loop along Marine Dr.
- 46.0 Pass Blue Lake Park. Continue on 40 Mile Loop route following the Columbia River.
- 51.0 Ends back at Glen Jackson Bridge.

13

Monster Cookie Challenge

Salem—St. Paul—Champoeg Park—Salem

The Monster Cookie ·Ride, sponsored each spring since 1974 by the Salem Bicycle Club, attracts more than five hundred riders who enjoy the 62-mile loop from Salem to Champoeg Park on beautiful rural roads. Along the way riders consume more than twenty-five hundred cookies, one thousand bananas, forty pounds of apples, and forty gallons of juice. Participants don't usually lose weight on this ride, but everybody has a great time. Riders of many abilities—from ten-year-old children to triathletes in training—share in the fun. The route provides an excellent way to explore farmland north of Salem any time of year. During spring the Willamette Valley blooms with colorful flowers, in summer you can sample a wide variety of berries, autumn brings on harvest activities, and even winter rides are possible, thanks to the valley's relatively mild climate.

The ride begins at the Willamette University Sparks Center in downtown Salem, the Oregon state capital. The city has the typical clean, orderly atmosphere of a state capital, with numerous manicured parks and historic buildings to explore. The Mission Mill Village, located just across 12th Street from the university, features a working turn-of-the-century water-powered wool mill, historic buildings, and a variety of craft shops that offer a taste of life in Salem's early days. Salem is an excellent city for bicycling, with its many miles of bicycle routes, paths, and footpaths to delight nonmotorized travelers. This route uses well-marked bike lanes through the city's old commercial district and out of town, making urban bicycling easy even for novices.

The Salem Parkway Bike Route becomes a separated path on the west side of the parkway at mile 3.7. You'll want to keep an eye out for the many pedestrians who also enjoy this paved path fenced off from the busy roadway and adjacent to green pastures. The pathway ends at Chemawa Road, where you'll follow Radiant Drive, a quiet, meandering road that parallels I–5 for 4 miles, and then cross to River Road (Highway 219). This moderately busy highway is a designated bike route with good, wide shoulders. In 5 miles Monster Cookie riders stop at the Nusom's Fruit Orchard for rest and refreshments. Nusom's fruit stand sells healthy treats, to bicyclists' delight.

The route continues on River Road through the small, but friendly, community of St. Louis, and over miles of flat farmland to beautiful Champoeg Park. This is the site of Oregon's first Provisional Government. Each July, the story of old Oregon is reenacted as part of the Champoeg Historic Pageant, with dozens of performers in period costumes using black-powder rifles, bagpipes, and bugles. The Salem Club uses the Oak Grove picnic area as a rest stop, where riders enjoy box lunches under shade trees.

The return route to Salem follows Arbor Grove and Manning roads, quiet and flat farm roads, then circles back to Nusom's Orchard on Highway 219. Monster Cookie riders often take a last rest there before the final leg of the ride, which retraces the Salem Parkway's separated bike path and uses bike lanes through downtown. They return to the Willamette University in a stream of tired but satisfied riders.

The Basics

Start: Willamette University Sparks Center, off Bellevue St. From I–5 take exit 253 to Hwy. 22 west, which becomes Mission St. Follow signs to Willamette University. The shorter, loop route runs from Nusom's Orchard, on Hwy. 219, to Champoeg Park and back.
Length: 62 or 29 miles.

Terrain: Mostly flat, good roads.

Food: Hopmere Market, at 10.7 and 51.3 miles; Nusom's Orchard fruit stand (in season), at 16.5 and 45.5 miles; and store and café in St. Paul, at 23.6 miles.

For more information: Salem Bicycle Club, P.O. Box 7666, Salem, OR 97303. Salem Convention and Visitors Association, 1313 Mill St. SE, Salem, OR 97301; (800) 874–7012 or (503) 581–4325.

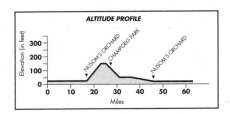

Miles & Directions

- 0.0 Exiting the Willamette University Sparks Center, turn right on Bellevue/Pringle Pkwy., which curves to become Ferry St., through the downtown commercial district.
- 1.0 Follow Ferry St. as it curves right to become Front St., parallel to the Willamette River. Follow Front north as it becomes Commercial and then Liberty St.
- 3.0 Turn right onto the Salem Pkwy. In 0.5 mile cross the parkway at Cherry Ave. to ride on the separated path. This path allows cyclists to avoid congestion around freeway on-ramps farther down the parkway.
- 6.6 Turn left on Chemawa Rd. at light, then right onto Radiant Dr. just before railroad tracks. This becomes a nice rural road that meanders parallel to I–5.
- 7.4 Turn right to stay on Radiant Dr., which becomes 35th Ave.
- 9.0 Turn left at stop sign on Quinaby Rd. Be careful crossing rough railroad tracks in 0.3 miles.
- 9.6 Turn right on River Rd. (Hwy. 219), a designated bike route.
- 10.7 Hopmere Market.

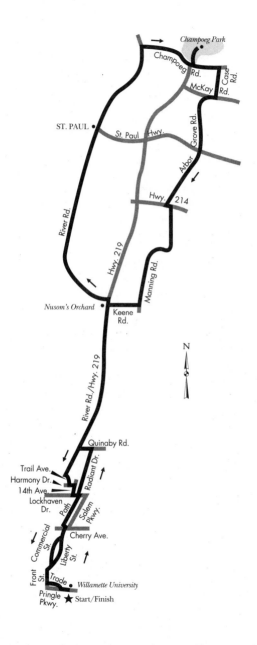

- 16.5 Turn left just past Nusom's Fruit Orchard to stay on River Rd., toward St. Paul and Newburg. *The shorter, 29-mile route begins and ends here, looping up to Champoeg Park.*
- 23.6 St. Paul.
- 27.7 Turn right onto Champoeg Rd.
- 30.1 Turn off to rest stop in Champoeg Park. If you don't stop here, subtract 1.8 miles from the rest of your distances.
- 31.9 Turn left from Champoeg Park onto Champoeg Rd.
- 32.9 Turn right on Case Rd.
- 34.2 Turn right on McKay Rd.
- 34.8 Turn left on Arbor Grove Rd.
- 40.0 Turn left onto Hwy. 214, then an immediate right to continue on Arbor Grove Rd., which becomes Manning Rd.
- 44.3 Turn right on Keene Rd., 0.5 mile past St. Louis Rd.
- 45.7 Turn left back onto River Rd., Hwy. 219, near Nusom's Fruit Orchard.
- 53.7 Turn left at first light, opposite McNary Estates, then a quick right at stop sign onto Trail Ave.
- 54.0 Turn left onto Harmony Dr., then right on 14th Ave. at stop sign, and a quick left onto Lockhaven Dr. at stoplight.
- 55.5 Turn right back onto the Salem Pkwy. Bike Path. Follow it back to Commercial St. and Front St.
- 61.2 Bear left onto Trade St., which becomes Pringle Pkwy.
- 62.0 End back at Willamette University Sparks Center.

Northern Willamette Valley

Covered Bridge Ramble and Crabtree Cruise

The Willamette Valley, big, flat, and fertile, fills much of north-west Oregon. The valley is full of dairy, grain, and vegetable farms, many of which date back to the last century. Small clusters of oak forest and bits of wild prairie hint of the natural beauty that must have existed centuries ago. The valley is a fine place to bicycle, with its mild climate, plenty of lightly traveled side roads, and lots of interesting destinations to visit. It presents a variety of faces: On a cool spring or autumn day, it is covered with gray mist, summer days can be shimmering hot, evening sunsets display oranges and reds across fields and through the silhouettes of trees. The cloudy weather and drizzly rain of winter bring calm.

The Mid-Valley Wheelmen of Corvallis sponsor an annual Covered Bridge Century, which explores many of the Willamette's best attractions. It's an enjoyable late-summer ride easily divided into two loops at the village of Crabtree. The town, .5 mile off the main highway, is little more than a few houses, the Crabtree Café and Tavern, and Dave's General Store. It's a nice starting point for these two rides, which emphasize the Willamette's rural beauty.

The shorter eastern loop includes plenty of wide open farmland, a stop in the small town of Scio, and five covered wooden bridges. Covered bridges, cleverly crafted and charming to look at, were built in the Willamette Valley during the turn of the century for the sake of farmers and ranchers who had trouble convincing cattle to cross open bridges, and to protect the wood from rotting in this damp climate. Although cattle now travel by truck and most new bridges are built of cement, the county continues, thank goodness, to maintain these traditional structures.

The 10-mile ride from Crabtree to the Larson Covered Bridge starts off flat, then encounters a few small hills. You can rest at the Larson Wayside Park, or go .5 mile farther to the larger Roaring River Park, which has freshwater. Both parks offer plenty of riverside shade trees and picnic tables. Heading north through dry, slightly hilly country, you'll cross Mill Creek on the Shimanek, and, a few miles later, the Hannah Covered Bridges. The route circles back, west on Highway 226, to the town of Scio. The Old Town Store there will be glad to satisfy your hunger and thirst. Heading south now, you'll soon encounter the only major climb of this ride, a 1-mile incline. At the top you are rewarded with a patchwork-quilt view of the valley. Turn right onto Hungry Hill Road at the bottom of the hill. You'll cross the Hoffman Covered Bridge over Beaver Creek, then return to Crabtree.

The longer western loop we call the Crabtree Cruise. The flatter option, it's an enjoyable ride that provides an excellent cross section of American life. You'll see old farmhouses with big oak or maple trees in the yard, often with a swing dangling from a high branch. Small creeks meander through the countryside, and scattered clumps of tall woods provide cool shade on hot days. Passing through Millersburg and historic districts in Albany, you'll see the proud homes of people who live and work in these industrial communities.

Covered Bridge Ramble

Crabtree—Larwood Wayside Park—Scio—Crabtree

The Basics

Start: Crabtree. To get to Crabtree take exit 233 from I–5, follow Hwy. 20 east 6 miles east, bear left onto Hwy. 226, go 8.1 miles, and turn left onto Cold Springs Rd. Go .5 mile north to Crabtree Rd., turn right, and 1 block east is the Crabtree Tavern.

Length: 35 miles.
Terrain: Mostly small rolling hills, some flat.
Food: Food is available at the Old Towne grocery in Scio, at 28.2 miles. Bring plenty to drink.
For more information: Mid-Valley Wheelmen, P.O. Box 1283, Corvallis, OR 97339.

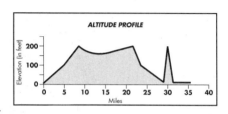

Miles & Directions

- 0.0 Head east toward the mountains on Crabtree Rd., and follow as the road curves south.
- 0.5 Turn left onto Hwy. 226.
- 1.8 Turn right onto Fish Hatchery Dr., just as the highway curves left.
- 8.2 Bear left at fork to continue on Fish Hatchery Dr.
- 8.5 Cross the Larwood Covered Bridge, then turn left onto Larwood Dr. You can rest at the Larwood Wayside Park at the corner, or ride .5 mile farther on Fish Hatchery Dr. to the Roaring River Park.
- 13.4 Turn right onto Richardson Gap Rd.
- 16.2 Cross Hwy. 226.
- 17.0 Cross the Shimanek Covered Bridge, then turn right onto Shimanek Bridge Dr.
- 19.0 Bear left into Hwy. 226.
- 21.4 Turn right onto Morrison Camp Rd. The Hannah Covered Bridge is straight ahead. After crossing this bridge, turn around. Turn left back onto Hwy. 226.
- 23.8 Bear left at Shimanek Bridge Dr. to continue on Hwy. 226.

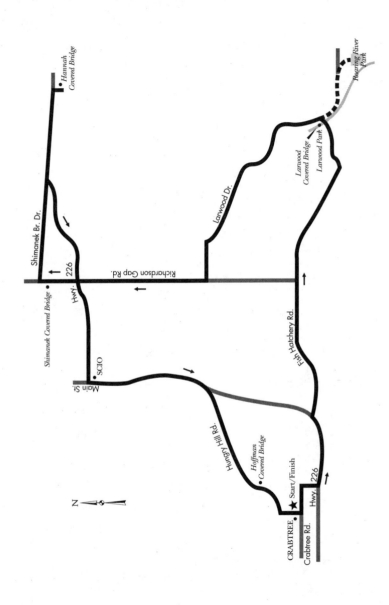

- 28.2 Enter Scio. Turn left at stop sign on Main St. to continue on Hwy. 226.
- 31.3 Turn right onto Hungry Hill Rd. *Watch out:* This turnoff is easy to miss!
- 33.8 Cross the Hoffman Covered Bridge over Beaver Creek.
- 35.0 Turn left on Crabtree Rd. End back in Crabtree.

Crabtree Cruise

Crabtree—Millersburg—Albany—Tangent—Crabtree

The Basics

Start: Crabtree. To get to Crabtree take exit 233 from I–5, follow Hwy. 20 6 miles east, bear left onto Hwy. 226, go 8.1 miles, turn left onto Cold Springs Rd. Go .5 mile, turn right on Crabtree Rd., and stop at the Crabtree Tavern.

Length: 58 miles.

Terrain: Mostly flat, agricultural lands. Roads are busy through Albany and on Hwy. 34 near Corvallis.

Food: Stores in Crabtree and in Jefferson, at 12.5 miles; several options in Millersburg, at 17 miles, and Albany, at 20 miles; Marv's Corner Store at 31 miles; and a café on Hwy. 99, just past Tangent Dr. at 39.3 miles.

For more information: Albany Visitors Association, P.O. Box 548, Albany, OR 97321; (800) 526–2256 and (541) 928–0911.

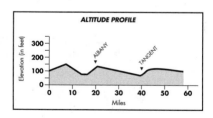

Miles & Directions

- 0.0 Head west on Crabtree Rd.
- 0.8 Turn right onto Gilkey Rd.
- 3.9 Turn right at Kelly Rd. to stay on Gilkey Rd.
- 4.3 Turn left to stay on Gilkey Rd. Continue on this road to the Gilkey Bridge over Thomas Creek, the only covered bridge on this route.
- 6.2 Turn left onto Robinson Dr.
- 7.2 Turn left onto Jefferson-Scio Dr.
- 10.1 Cross the North Santiam River.
- 12.5 Enter Jefferson. Turn left onto Hwy. 99E.
- 14.6 Cross under I–5. Continue following the road as it curves left to become the Old Salem Hwy. Ride through Millersburg, a community of wood and paper mills.
- 17.6 Follow the road as it curves left and goes under railroad tracks. Immediately turn right, before road goes under the freeway.
- 19.3 Waverly Park is to your left.
- 20.1 Rough railroad tracks, so cross carefully!
- 20.6 Turn left at stop sign onto Main St., then take an immediate right onto 3rd Ave. Follow this through the Hackleman and Monteith historic districts of Albany.
- 21.7 Ride past the City of Albany Water Treatment Plant, then cross the Calapooia River into Bryant Park. Continue on the same road, which is now called Bryant Dr., as it zigzags through farmland.
- 23.8 Turn left to stay on Bryant Dr.
- 24.3 Turn right at stop sign onto Riverside Dr.
- 29.0 Turn left at old cemetery on Orleans Rd., in 0.2 mile turn right onto Hwy. 34. This is a busy highway, especially during rush hour, but has a good wide shoulder.
- 31.6 Turn left at traffic light onto Peoria Rd.
- 34.4 Turn left onto Tangent Dr.
- 39.3 Turn right onto Hwy. 99E. In 0.1 mile take a quick left to continue east on Tangent Dr.
- 42.1 Cross over I–5.

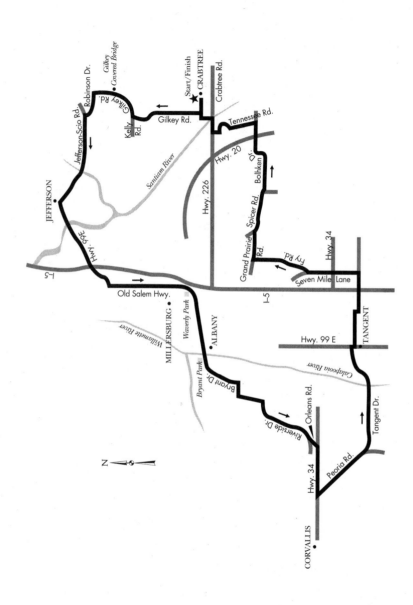

- 42.6 Turn left onto Seven Mile Lane.
- 44.7 Bear right onto Fry Rd.
- 47.4 Turn right onto Grand Prairie Rd.
- 48.6 Bear right onto Spicer Rd.
- 50.1 Follow Spicer Rd. as it curves right, then turn left onto Bolhken Dr. Continue on this road as it zigzags left then right.
- 53.3 Cross Hwy. 20, as road becomes Honey Sign Rd.
- 53.8 Turn left onto Tennessee Rd.
- 56.1 Turn right onto Hwy. 226. Cross the beautiful South Santiam River.
- 57.6 Turn left on Cold Springs Rd., follow sign toward Crabtree.
- 58.0 Turn right on Crabtree Rd. End back at Crabtree Tavern.

16

Eugene Ramble

Alton Baker Park—Willamette River Bike Path
Island Park—Alton Baker Park

Eugene, Oregon is one of the most bicycle-friendly cities in the United States. Visitors are often amazed at the many miles of bicycle lanes, the enjoyable paths, and the sheer number of people who bicycle for transportation and recreation. During a typical rush hour you are likely to see a steady flow of bicyclists weaving through traffic, dressed in everything from business suits to Lycra tights. For more than a decade, Eugene has been recognized as a leader in encouraging bicycle riding. The city employs a bicycle coordinator who oversees facility construction, mapping, and bicycle events and programs. Eugene residents take pride in their community's commitment to bicycling.

In fact, the entire state of Oregon has shown leadership in bicycle planning and encouragement. A 1971 "Bikeway Bill" dedicates one percent of state fuel-tax receipts to bicycle facilities and footpaths. Most cities in the state now have growing bikeway systems. Of course there were howls from the automobile industry when this law was introduced. As it turned out, everybody, including motor vehicle users, has benefited since increased bicycling reduces traffic congestion and pollution and frees parking space for drivers. In the years since that law was passed, bicycle and pedestrian encouragement programs have become a normal part of traffic planning under the concept of "transportation demand management." The Pacific Northwest has become a leader in this economically efficient and environmentally responsible approach to transportation planning.

Bicycling reigns on the Eugene Ramble. The ride follows the Willamette River bicycle path system, which connects riverfront parks, recreation centers, and the University of Oregon between the cities of Springfield and Eugene. There are paths on both sides of the river and four bridges reserved exclusively for pedestrians and bicyclists. Along it you will experience the joys of bicycling and the charms of a well-landscaped city that maintains abundant green space within walking distance of downtown. The last part of this ride, between Alton Baker Park in Eugene and Island Park in Springfield is one of the nicest. The path winds through dense woods, along churning river rapids, and through a pleasant Springfield neighborhood.

Of course, it's important to follow special precautions for safety and courtesy when bicycling on multiuse trails, which you'll be sharing with pedestrians, joggers, skaters, and bicyclists of all ages and abilities. Pass slower walkers and bicyclists on the left, after giving a friendly verbal warning. Ride single file unless there is plenty of room, and be sure to get completely off the trail whenever you stop to avoid congestion.

The Basics

Start: Alton Baker Park, on the north bank of the Willamette River in Eugene. From I–5 take I–105 toward Eugene, exit at Coburg Rd. (toward Autzen Stadium), turn right on Country Club, take the first left, go under the roadway, then take the first right into the park.

Length: Basic ride is 17.5 miles. Shorter and longer variations are possible.

Terrain: Flat.

Food: There are opportunities to buy snacks at several points along this route, or bring a picnic lunch to enjoy at Island Park.

For more information: Eugene Bicycle Program, 858 Pearl St., Eugene OR 97401; phone (541) 687–5298, fax (541) 687–5598. For

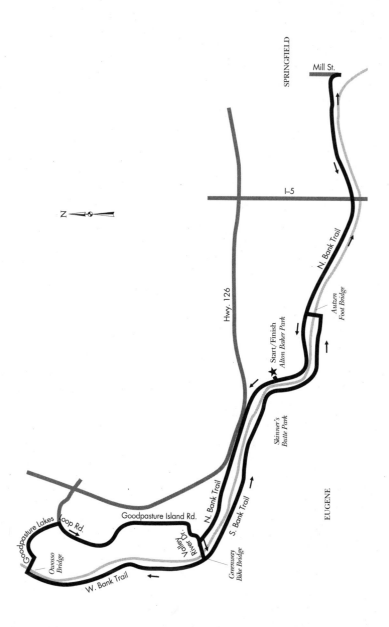

an ambitious ride, contact the Eugene/Springfield Visitors Bureau (800–547–5445 or 541–484–5307) for a free copy of the Willamette Valley Bicycle Scenic Map, which describes a multiday cycling adventure "through the Heart of Oregon."

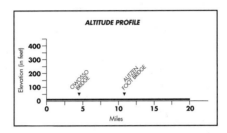

Miles & Directions

- 0.0 Turn right on the N. Bank Trail.
- 2.5 Turn left onto the Greenway Bike Bridge across the river, then turn right onto the W. Bank Trail.
- 4.5 Turn right to cross Owosso Bridge. Follow the bikeway left along Goodpasture Lake Loop Rd.
- 5.5 Turn right onto Goodpasture Island Rd.
- 8.0 Turn right onto Valley River Dr., then follow the path back across the Greenway Bike Bridge, and turn left onto the S. Bank Trail.
- 11.0 Turn left to cross the Autzen Foot Bridge, then right on the N. Bank Trail.
- 14.0 Turn right on Mill St. and stop at Springfield's Island Park. Turn around; return on N. Bank Trail to Alton Baker Park.
- 17.5 End.

Mount Bachelor Classic

Sunriver—Deschutes National Forest
Elk Lake—Mt. Bachelor—Sunriver

Central Oregon is a land filled with the aroma of pine forests and sage, sparkling rivers descending from snow-capped volcanic mountains, and people who maintain the cowpoke's enjoyment of the outdoor life. It is a semiarid country that has a lot to offer visitors. This ride through beautiful forests, past brilliant lakes, and up to the base of spectacular Mount Bachelor is highly recommended. The route presented here is the nicest part of the Sunnyside Century, a late-summer ride sponsored since 1971 by the Alpenglow Bicycle Club of Bend, Oregon. We have modified the ride to begin at the Sunriver Village resort, which avoids the heavy traffic of Highway 97.

Sunriver is a destination resort, which means that a variety of recreational activities is available to visitors. Bicycling is one of the most popular. The resort itself has more than 30 miles of bike paths, and there are numerous excellent riding opportunities in the area. The largely undeveloped Deschutes National Forest offers miles of low-traffic roads and excellent off-road bicycling. The three bicycle shops in Sunriver will gladly rent bicycles.

The ride heads west from Sunriver on Three Trappers Road (Forest Service Road no. 40) through the Deschutes National Forest. Usually there isn't much traffic on this road. It's an ideal route if you enjoy privacy while bicycling; you'll have the forest, big blue sky, and your own thoughts for company for 20 miles. There's beauty everywhere you look. You may want to explore an unpaved side road or hike a creek-side trail for close-up sights and smells of the pine forest. Mount Bachelor occasionally glances down from afar. As you ride through this region, you'll notice remnants of volcanic activity, from the various lava-dome peaks (Cultus Mountain beckons straight ahead) to the many textures and colors of rock and soil. The quiet and calm that you experience now contrasts sharply with the violent eruptions that have swept through this region.

Soon after crossing the Deschutes River (actually more of a creek at this point), which flows from the Little Lava Lake on your right to the Crane Prairie Reservoir on your left, you'll join the Cascade Lakes Highway. Head north, following the river, to Lava Lake. Continue to Elk Lake, a lovely spot for swimming or a rest. Stop at the public park at the southern end, or visit the Elk Lake Resort for lunch at the inviting little café and store. You may want to return another time to explore the lake by boat (available for rent at the resort), but today you'll probably need to save energy for bicycling.

Continuing north, you begin to encounter the climbs that make this route a challenge and the increasingly breathtaking scenery that makes it so rewarding. You can cool off halfway up with a swim at Devils Lake. After a small climb the valley opens into a beautiful vista of Sparks Lake sitting in a big grassy plain with Mt. Bachelor in the background. From there it's a sometimes steep climb farther up the mountain, past the famous ski resort. Your reward is 5 miles of fast descent down the mountain slope, another 5 miles of gradual descent through the forest, and an easy final leg back to Sunriver Village.

The Basics

Start: Sunriver Village parking lot. Sunriver is 17 miles south of Bend, 2 miles west of Hwy. 97.

Length: 64.0 miles.

Terrain: Some flat, some rolling hills, and a few major climbs. Roads are in good condition, with generally light traffic.

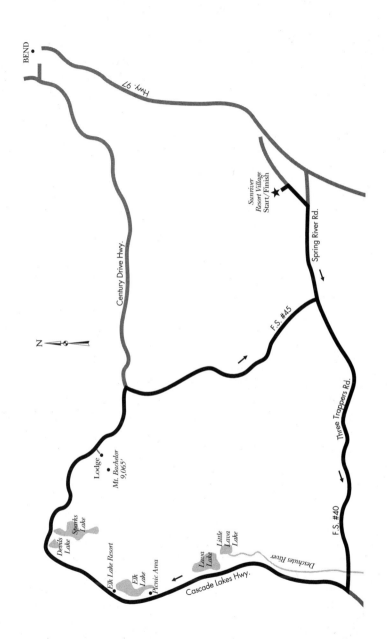

Food: The only food and water is at the Elk Lake Resort, at 33.2 miles. Although the route crosses several streams, drinking untreated water is not recommended.

For more information: Alpenglow Velo Bike Club, Box 6738, Bend, OR 97708. Bike map and other information available from Deschutes County Public Works, 61150 SE 27th St., Bend, OR 97702; (541) 388–6581.

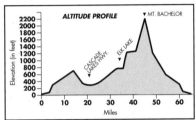

Miles & Directions

- 0.0 Leave Sunriver Village, turn right on main road (Cottonwood Dr., which becomes Spring River Rd.).
- 3.0 Enter Deschutes National Forest, and continue on Three Trappers Rd. (Forest Service Rd. no. 40).
- 21.0 Turn right onto the Cascade Lakes Hwy. Follow the Deschutes River for several miles.
- 30.5 Elk Lake public picnic area.
- 33.2 Elk Lake Resort turnoff. (The café and store here is your only food stop on this ride.)
- 37.2 Road curves around beautiful Devils Lake. A little farther is the major climb of this ride to the base of Mt. Bachelor. Hang in there!
- 44.2 Turnoff to Mt. Bachelor Lodge. Facilities are closed during summer. Descent begins, so check your brakes!
- 47.3 Turn right onto Forest Service Rd. no. 45 (don't miss this turnoff or you'll end up in Bend). The steep descent continues.
- 59.2 Turn left onto Forest Service Rd. no. 40.
- 61.5 Exit Deschutes National Forest.
- 64.0 Turn left, end back at Sunriver Resort.

18

Crater Lake Cruise

North Junction—Steel Center
Rim Village—North Junction

Crater Lake is a spectacular jewel set in the volcanic caldera (cone) of Mount Mazama in south-central Oregon. The lake water is a deep blue, changing shades as the sun changes its angle in the sky. This ride is both extremely exhilarating and challenging. Although only 33 miles in length, the road encircling the rim is a series of steep climbs and descents, sweeping up and down more than 800 feet.

The lake surface itself is at an altitude of 6,176 feet, with a maximum depth of almost 2,000 feet. Sitting in the lake is Wizard Island, its tree-covered beauty doubled by the water's reflection. Along the shore is an endless variety of shapes and textures sculpted into rock by volcanic action. The volcanic activity that formed Crater Lake created numerous fascinating geologic formations, including cinder cones and lava flows of various sizes and colors.

Bicycling around the lake on the Rim Road offers excellent views, both inward toward the lake and outward to the beautiful countryside of south-central Oregon. The National Park Service provides interpretive signs at numerous viewpoints. Along the way you can hike to fire lookout towers or down to the lake itself at Cleetwood Cove. During the summer tour boats circle the lake and stop at Wizard Island. The National Park Service's Steel Information Center, near the junction with the south entrance road, is worth a visit to learn about the park's history and geography. The Crater Lake Lodge, which includes a store and restaurant, has the rustic charm of traditional stone and log park facilities. For reservations at the lodge, call (541) 594–2511.

Crater Lake Park includes subalpine old-growth forests of lodgepole pine, mountain hemlock, Shasta red fir, whitebark pine, and Nobel fir. There are more than 100 miles of trails within the park, including several along the Rim Road. Park rangers offer talks and tours, which highlight the park's natural history. Check at Steel Center Park Headquarters for specific information.

Crater Lake National Park is a popular tourist destination, which means that bicyclists must share the roadway with numerous recreational vehicles. Fortunately, nobody is in a hurry. Bicycling is best early in the morning or in off-peak season to avoid the busiest traffic. Bicyclists should be courteous to other users by allowing faster vehicles to pass on the hills. The eastern section of Rim Drive tends to have less traffic. It is usually closed from early October through late June due to snow.

The Basics

Start: You can start either from the North Junction parking lot or the park headquarters at the south end.
Length: The loop totals a challenging 33 miles.
Terrain: There is little flat surface on the Rim Dr. Inclines average 5 percent. Roads are relatively narrow but generally in good repair.
Food: The only food and water is at Rim Village or at Mazama Campground. Take plenty to drink and eat for the strenuous ride.
For more information: Crater Lake National Park, P.O. Box 7, Crater Lake, OR 97604; (541) 594–2211.

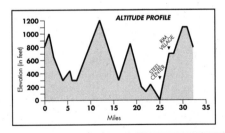

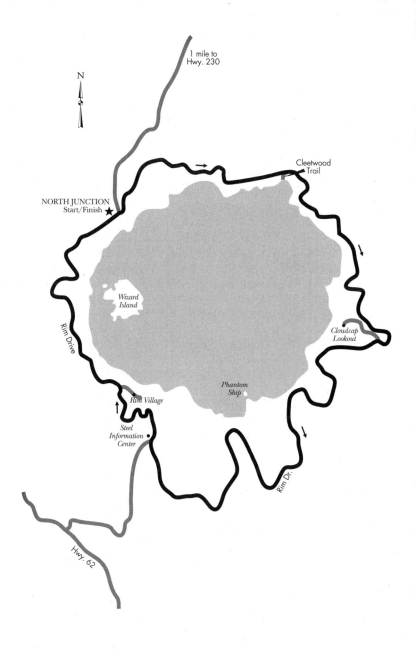

1 mile to
Hwy. 230

N

Cleetwood
Trail

NORTH JUNCTION
Start/Finish

Wizard
Island

Cloudcap
Lookout

Rim Drive

Rim Village

Phantom
Ship

Steel
Information
Center

Rim Dr.

Hwy. 62

19

Sams Valley Cruise

Gold Hill—Sams Valley—Wimer
Rogue River—Gold Hill

The Sams Valley Cruise is a beautiful ride through the valleys, forests, and hills of southern Oregon. Recommended by Mark and Jean Chinn of Ashland's Siskiyou Wheelmen Bicycle Club, it is one of the club's most popular day rides. Mark and Jean suggest riding it during the region's mild spring and fall weather, when bicyclists can peel down to shorts and a light jersey and won't suffer from the midsummer heat.

The ride starts in Gold Hill, a small community on the Rogue River between the cities of Medford and Grants Pass. Following the Sams Valley Highway past orchards and small farms along the Rogue River, the route continues north through a vast open meadow covered with farms and cattle ranches, then past the Upper and Lower Table Rocks on the appropriately named Meadow Road. Along this road you climb steadily into the higher oak and pine forests, and from a summit you'll enjoy spectacular views back into the Rogue River Valley. If the day is clear, you can look over a vast carpet of green farms and forests to Mount McLoughlin, 30 miles east.

There's an easy descent to Evans Creek Road, a low-traffic road that meanders over rolling hills. Bicyclists often have the whole road to themselves. Follow Evans Creek to the community of Wimer. The historical covered bridge east of town is a pleasant rest spot, and riders usually buy snacks at the Wimer Market.

From Wimer the most enjoyable route to Rogue River is the West Evans Creek Road, which has little automobile traffic. In Rogue River the route turns left on Main Street, then follows North River Road for a pleasant and easy return to Gold Hill.

There are many other activities for visitors in this part of Oregon. You may want to combine bicycling with a visit to the world-famous Ashland Shakespeare Festival or take advantage of excellent off-road bicycling in the Siskiyou and Rogue River national forests.

The Basics

Start: Gold Hill city park at 2nd Ave. and 4th St. Gold Hill is a small town off exit 35 on I–5, halfway between Grants Pass and Medford.

Length: 49.4 miles.

Terrain: Rolling hills with some flat and one 600-foot climb on Meadow Rd.

Food: Gold Hill Market at start; Wimer Market at 31.4 miles; store, Bruno's Pizza, and Doughnut Hut in Rogue River, at 41.4 miles.

For more information: Siskiyou Wheelmen, P.O. Box 974, Ashland, OR 97520. Ashland Visitors Information, 110 E. Main St., Ashland, OR 97520; (541) 482–3486.

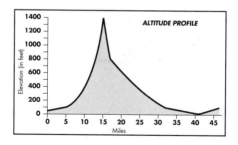

Miles & Directions

- 0.0 Go east on 4th Ave. Follow the road as it curves left along the Rogue River to become Sams Valley Hwy., Hwy. 234. Green highway sign reads SAMS VALLEY, CRATER LAKE.
- 2.2 Gold Nugget State Park.
- 6.3 Continue on Hwy. 234; do not take the Old Sams Valley Hwy.
- 8.3 Turn left on Table Rock Rd.
- 9.3 Turn left on Meadow Rd.
- 17.2 Turn left onto E. Evans Creek Rd.
- 31.4 Historical covered bridge to your left. Cross this bridge to visit rustic outhouses (with DOE and BUCK signs to indicate women's and men's).
- 32.0 Ride through Wimer, turn left on E. Evans Creek Rd.
- 32.3 Turn right on W. Evans Creek Rd., in 0.5 mile turn left on Pine Grove Rd.
- 33.8 Cross Manthorne Rd., staying on Pine Grove Rd.
- 35.1 Turn left on W. Evans Creek Rd.
- 40.5 Palmerton Arboretum, adjacent to Evans Creek.
- 40.8 Bear left onto Foothills Rd.
- 41.1 Enter the town of Rogue River. Turn right, then immediately left onto Main St.
- 41.5 Follow Main St. right into N. River Rd.
- 47.2 Bear left at stop sign to continue on N. River Rd.
- 49.4 End back in Gold Hill.

Eastern Washington

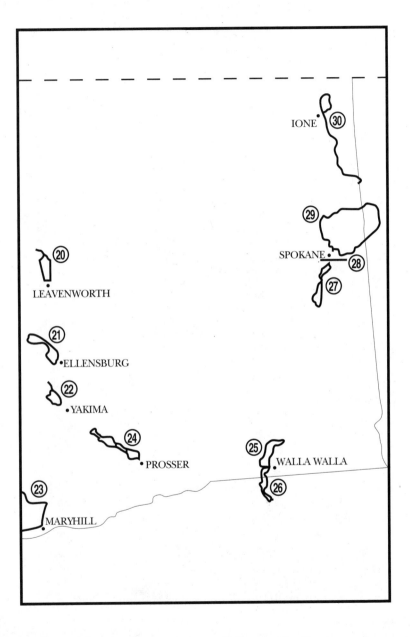

IONE ⑳

㉙

SPOKANE · ㉘

㉗

⑳
LEAVENWORTH

㉑
·ELLENSBURG

㉒
· YAKIMA

㉔
· PROSSER

㉕
WALLA WALLA

㉖

㉓
MARYHILL

Eastern Washington

20

Leavenworth Cruise

Leavenworth—Plain—Lake Wenatchee
Coles Corner—Leavenworth

This route is the best part of the annual Apple Century, a major ride sponsored by the Wenatchee Sunrise Rotary that is held late each spring. It's an exhilarating ride through gorgeous Cascade Mountain valleys. The scenery alone will take your breath away, and the route includes a steady climb and hairpin descent.

The ride begins in Leavenworth, a tourist community on Highway 2. Leavenworth displays the worst and best of tourism. It began as a railroad and mill town at the end of the nineteenth century but was bypassed by a new railway line in the 1920s and fell into hard times. Now it's a Bavarian "theme" town. Buildings are decorated with gingerbread trim, store clerks wear costumes, and numerous boutiques sell overpriced knickknacks. But if you tire of this tackiness, there are many great opportunities for outdoor recreation: skiing, hiking, river rafting, fishing, sailboarding, and, of course, bicycling. The town is surrounded by beautiful snowcapped mountains, forests, and orchards. The incredibly clean air and water are rejuvenating to city visitors.

The first third of the ride through narrow, winding mountain valleys is so pleasant you may hardly notice that you are climbing. The higher you get, the better the views of the valley behind you and the mountains ahead. Only the last couple of miles of ascent feel steep. Just when climbing becomes really hard, you reach the summit, then zigzag steeply down to the community of Plain.

It's level riding from there to Lake Wenatchee. The optional section along Lake Wenatchee's North Shore Road is highly recommended for its beautiful views and a chance to lunch at the Cougar Inn.

There's more level riding on Highway 207 to Coles Corner at the junction with Highway 2. This highway is busier than the first portion of the route, but it has good shoulders, and you'll enjoy a steady descent back to Leavenworth. After a day of bicycling, you'll appreciate the town's abundant food and entertainment.

The Basics

Start: Downtown Leavenworth, on Hwy. 2, in the Washington Cascades.

Length: 38.5 miles, or 49 miles with the detour along Lake Wenatchee.

Terrain: A steady but easy climb during the first quarter of the ride, level or descents from there on.

Food: Wiley Coyote Deli in Plain, at 14.5 miles; store and Squirrel Tree Inn Restaurant at Coles Corner, at 23.4 miles; Cougar Inn Restaurant on Lake Wenatchee; Happy Clown Restaurant at the foot of Lake Wenatchee.

For more information: Leavenworth Chamber of Commerce, P.O. Box 327, Leavenworth, WA 98826; (509) 548–5807. Apple Century, P.O. Box 1433, Wenatchee, WA 98801.

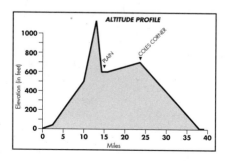

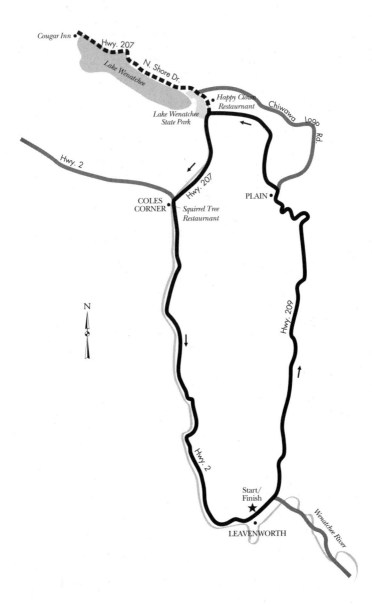

Cougar Inn

Hwy. 207

N. Shore Dr.

Lake Wenatchee

Happy Cloud Restaurant

Chiwawa Loop Rd.

Lake Wenatchee State Park

Hwy. 2

Hwy. 207

COLES CORNER

Squirrel Tree Restaurant

PLAIN

N

Hwy. 209

Hwy. 2

Start/ Finish

Wenatchee River

LEAVENWORTH

Miles & Directions

- 0.0 From the Gazebo in downtown Leavenworth, ride east on Hwy. 2.
- 0.5 Turn left on Hwy. 209 at the fork just outside of town. Continue as this road zigzags toward Plain.
- 14.5 Pass through the community of Plain. Follow Hwy. 209 left.
- 19.6 Turn left on Hwy. 207.

  Turn right for an optional side trip on N. Shore Dr. along Lake Wenatchee.

- 23.4 Turn left on Hwy. 2 at Coles Corner.
- 38.5 End back in Leavenworth.

21

Manastash Challenge

Ellensburg—Thorp—Cle Elum—Ellensburg

Early autumn is an ideal time of year to explore the Kittitas Valley, which lies just east of the towering Cascades in central Washington State. Although there is often snow on the mountains by that time of year, the valley usually has relatively mild weather. The Manastash Metric Fall Colors Tour, sponsored by the Ellensburg Cross-Country Ski Club, is timed to take advantage of this climate. The ride is named for the extraordinary Manastash Ridge of peaks to the southwest of the Ellensburg Valley.

The Manastash Metric, held the second Saturday of October, is one of the last major annual bicycle events of the year in the Pacific Northwest bicycle-events calendar. The majority of riders come from Puget Sound communities, where autumn rains have already begun. The route, which hasn't changed for more than a decade, is ideal for exploring this beautiful valley of ranches and timber communities, making use of low traffic and relatively flat roads.

The ride starts from Ellensburg, the largest city in the region and home of Central Washington University. Ellensburg has a charming old downtown of turn-of-the-century buildings, an ideal place to stretch your legs and buy snacks in preparation for the day's ride. Soon after leaving the city, you cross the Yakima River and ride through the small cattle, horse, and sheep ranches that fill much of the Kittatas Valley.

Interstate 90 cuts through the valley. You'll cross over the highway to the small unincorporated community of Thorp. A little farther the route forks. There you can either continue on to Cle Elum for the full 100-kilometer ride or choose the easier 50-kilometer route.

If you are taking the long route, you'll follow Taneum Road, past the ranch of Stuart Anderson (founder of the Black Angus restaurant chain), to a region of rolling foothills along the valley's southwest edge called Thorp Prairie. The next stretch offers some of the best views. You'll climb several hundred feet over the next few miles, to a high point of Elk Heights at 2,359 feet above sea level.

On one windy hilltop you'll pass by a 100-foot-tall "eggbeater" wind generator, an experimental device built to test commercial production of electricity by wind energy. To the right you'll see Lookout Mountain; to your left is the South Cle Elum Ridge, which includes Peoh Point. You'll follow Upper Peoh Point Road for several miles as it crosses and recrosses the Main Canal, one of several irrigation canals that supply valley farmers with fresh mountain water.

The ride descends to Cle Elum, an old coal-mining town now popular with tourists driving I–90. This is the halfway point and an ideal place to break for lunch. Don't miss the 1906 Cle Elum Bakery, a standard stop for bicyclists. For an enjoyable side trip, continue 4 miles northeast to the town of Roslyn, another old coal-mining town, which, being off the beaten track, has retained much of its historic character.

First Street, Cle Elum's main business district, becomes Highway 10, which heads back to Ellensburg. To avoid traffic congestion at the interstate intersection, you'll take Airport Road and pick up Highway 10 again along the Yakima River Canyon. The road hugs the canyon side, twisting sharply with the rushing river to one side and the grass-covered hills to the other. Combined with the background of forested mountains, you'll enjoy beautiful sights and an exciting ride.

Eventually the Yakima River Canyon opens back into the Kittitas Valley. There the 50-kilometer route rejoins for the descent to the valley floor. Turning off Highway 10, you ride through a stretch of lovely farms, up a short but steep climb on Hungry Junction Road, and back into Ellensburg.

The Basics

Start: Ellensburg Public Safety Building (police and fire station) at 2nd and Pearl sts., in downtown Ellensburg.

Length: 50 or 100 kilometers (32.2 or 64.2 miles), with a possible 10-mile side trip to the historic town of Roslyn.

Terrain: The 50-kilometer ride, through the Kittitas Valley, is flat except for one .5-mile climb after the second Yakima River crossing. The 100-kilometer ride has several short climbs between Thorp and Cle Elum, and back along the Yakima River Canyon.

Food: Store and deli at the I–90 crossing, at 10.4 miles; in Thorp, at 11.5 miles; and a variety of restaurants, stores, and a bakery in Cle Elum, at 32.5 miles.

For more information: Ellensburg Tourist Information, 436 N. Sprague St., Ellensburg, WA 98926; (509) 925–3137.

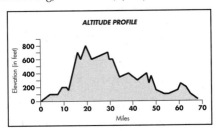

Miles & Directions

- 0.0 Head west on 2nd Ave. 1 block, then turn left onto Main St. This artery has a wide shoulder marked with a bike lane.
- 1.0 Turn right onto Uptaneum Rd. This takes you westward, out of town. In .7 mile you cross under I–90.
- 2.1 Pass the Irene Rinehart River Front Park entrance, cross the Yakima River, then turn right onto Brown Rd. on the opposite bank.
- 3.2 Turn right at T intersection, to continue on Brown Rd.
- 5.0 Turn right onto Hanson, then an immediate left onto the Thorp Hwy., which crosses over I–90. Just past I–90 you pass the

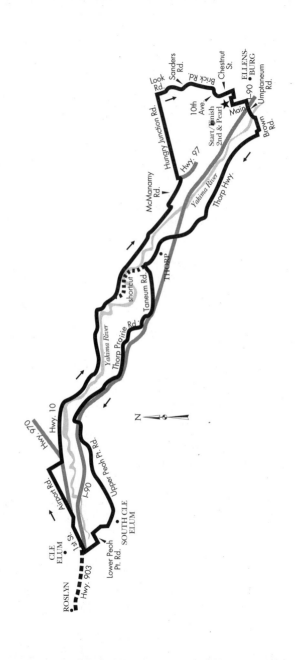

Iron Horse State Park, an abandoned railroad line that now serves as a 300-mile public trail.

- 11.5 Pass through the community of Thorp. Follow the road left as it zigzags just past the Thorp Store.
- 12.9 Turn left onto Taneum Rd., which takes you into rolling hills covered with huge cattle ranches.

For the shorter, 50-kilometer option, continue on Thorp Hwy., which becomes Hayward Rd. In 2.0 miles you cross the Yakima River on a narrow metal bridge, then climb for 1 mile up the side of the valley. Turn right onto Hwy. 10 to rejoin the 100-kilometer route.

- 14.0 Bear right, as Taneum becomes Thorp Prairie Rd., which follows I–90.
- 15.6 Climb small hill, then turn right to stay on Thorp Prairie Rd. just before the freeway overpass. Climb to Elk Height, the high point of this ride.
- 23.6 Cross over I–90, road becomes Upper Peoh Pt. Rd. The road follows the Main Canal, which you cross and recross twice. After the fourth canal crossing, you will descend into the Cle Elum valley.
- 29.5 Bear right and then left to stay on Upper Peoh Pt. Rd.
- 30.5 Turn left onto Lower Peoh Pt. Rd., which takes a quick descent through South Cle Elum. Follow the road as it crosses under I–90, then merge into Cle Elum's busy 1st St.

To visit the historic town of Roslyn, turn left on any cross street in downtown Cle Elum, and then left again on 2nd Ave., which becomes Hwy. 903 west. Return on the same road. This side trip adds about 10 miles to your ride.

- 33.8 Turn left, then an immediate right onto Cle Elum Airport Rd. This allows you to avoid the busy traffic interchanges on Hwy. 10 just outside of town.
- 36.7 Continue straight onto Masterson Rd.
- 37.4 Turn left onto Hwy. 970, and in 0.1 mile bear right onto Hwy. 10. Follow this road along the Yakima River Canyon for the next 15 miles.

- 52.5 Turn left onto McManamy Rd.
- 54.5 Turn left onto Hwy. 97.
- 55.0 Turn right onto Hungry Junction Rd. Continue straight, up a 0.5-mile climb to the upper plateau.
- 59.3 Turn right onto Look Rd. at T intersection.
- 61.1 Turn left at T onto Sanders Rd. Follow this road as it curves right to become Brick Rd.
- 62.5 Turn right at the bottom of a short decline onto 10th Ave., a busy city street. Tenth becomes Euclid.
- 62.8 Turn left onto Chestnut St. (Central Washington University campus sits on the other side of Chestnut.)
- 63.5 After climbing a small hill, turn right onto Capitol Ave.
- 64.1 Turn right onto Pearl St.
- 64.2 End back at Public Safety Building parking lot.

22

Naches Ramble

Indian Painted Rocks—Naches
Wenas Lake—Indian Painted Rocks

The small, orchard-filled Naches (Nah-cheese) Valley sits at the base of the Cascade Mountains, just northwest of Yakima. Highway 12 now runs along the Naches River, down the valley's center, leaving the old highways at the valley's sides for local traffic. This route, which loops around the valley on the older highways, is one of the most popular bike rides in the Yakima area. It is recommended by Svend's Sport Shop in Yakima.

No matter when you ride, the Naches Valley fruit orchards offer sensual delights to bicyclists. In spring bright and fragrant blossoms shower the road from a dozen different fruits and fruit varieties, each with a distinctive color and smell. Blocks of various trees bloom in a progression that starts with orchards in the lower valley and moves up to higher levels as the season progresses.

During summer cherries, apples, pears, and peaches dangle in the sun. On hot days an intoxicating mixture of fruity smells from the orchards mingles with the spicy odor of sage plants growing on the hillsides. The orchards offer bicyclists shade from the brilliant sunlight, while the occasional sprinkle of irrigation systems that accidentally spray the roadway provides a cooling treat.

In late summer and autumn, the trees are heavy with fruit, and the orchards are busy with the business of picking. There is a sense of urgency, and cyclists should take care not to block the trucks carrying huge bins of peaches, pears, and apples. After harvest the leaves turn color and fall, leaving a few forgotten fruit on the stark branches to sway in the breeze. Hearty bicyclists who ride in winter can meditate on the tremendous fertility hidden within the quiet, cold valley.

This ride starts from Indian Painted Rocks, where a short hike up the hillside trail leads to ancient petroglyphs and beautiful views of the valley. The route follows South Naches Road, which winds between the Naches River and the valley's southwest side. This is a designated bike route, so you will be greeted with a series of WATCH FOR BICYCLISTS signs. In 5 miles you will pass Eschbach County Park, where local families relax by picnicking on the riverbank.

The route continues up the valley, through orchards, to the town of Naches on Highway 12. Most of the town's businesses sprawl along the highway, but if you take time to explore the town itself, you'll find a pleasant community. Leaving town you follow the Old Naches Highway along the Naches Wapatox Canal, part of the Yakima region's extensive irrigation system.

Above the Naches Valley are sagebrush-covered hills, cut by numerous smaller valleys and gullies. A side trip recommended as part of this route is lunch at Wenas Lake Resort Café, just below the Wenatchee National Forest. This side trip begins just past the town of Naches with a challenging 250-foot climb and continues past cattle ranches and grain fields along Wenas Creek. After lunch you'll enjoy a pleasant, cooling descent.

The Old Naches Highway offers more great views as the road climbs slightly above some of the valley's most fertile orchards. This becomes Old Stage Road on the way back to Highway 12. For the final stretch, either ride on the shoulder of the busy highway, or cross as a pedestrian and take Powerhouse Road back to Indian Painted Rocks Monument.

The Basics

Start: Indian Painted Rocks. Take Hwy. 12 west from Yakima. At the 199 milepost, turn left on Acklay Rd., then an immediate right onto W. Powerhouse Rd. Park on the road shoulder near the large sign.

Length: 21.5 miles, or 40 miles with side trip to Wenas Lake.

Terrain: Hilly ride, but no major climbs. Light to moderate traffic.

Food: Stores and fast food in Naches, at 10.5 miles.

For more information: Yakima Valley Visitor and Convention Center, 10 N. 8th St., Yakima, WA 98901; (509) 575–1300.

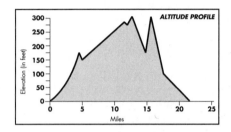

Miles & Directions

- 0.0 Head north on Powerhouse Rd.
- 0.3 Bear left at fork onto S. Naches Rd. Do not cross river.
- 5.1 Pass Eschbach County Park.
- 9.7 Continue straight at stop sign onto Naches-Tieton Rd.
- 10.2 Cross Naches River and then Hwy. 12. You are now in the town of Naches.
- 10.7 Turn right at the Gazebo, onto 2nd St. The town center, with additional shops, is to your left.
- 11.0 Bear left at Y. The road becomes Old Naches Hwy.
- 11.7 Continue straight, past powerhouse on the right. Stay on highway as it curves along the side of the valley.

For an enjoyable but challenging 20-mile side trip, turn left here onto Wenas Rd. In 5.5 miles, after a 250-foot climb, turn left onto N. Wenas Rd. In another 4.0 miles you will reach Wenas Lake, where you can stop for lunch at the Wenas Lake Resort Café, or enjoy a picnic at the public fishing dock.

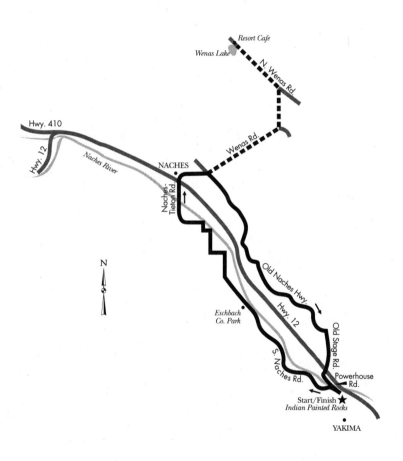

- 19.1 Follow road as it curves right and becomes Old Stage Road.
- 20.4 Turn left onto Hwy. 12, or, to avoid traffic, cross the highway as a pedestrian and turn left onto Powerhouse Rd. at the opposite side. Powerhouse Rd. parallels Hwy. 12.
- 21.5 End back at Indian Painted Rocks.

23

Gorge Challenge

Maryhill—Goldendale—Klickitat
Lyle—Horsethief Lake—Maryhill

The Columbia River Gorge is one of the most magnificent natural features in the Pacific Northwest. The gorge, more than 1,000 feet deep, cuts through the high prairie of eastern Washington and Oregon. It's a region of geologic drama and cultural diversity. The rolling hills are covered with farms, ranches, and timberlands, peopled with the rough-and-tough workers on which such traditional industries depend. The gorge, with towering sandstone cliffs and water sparkling under a steady wind and sun, offers spectacular vistas. It's a popular tourist destination, with a variety of recreational attractions to enjoy.

Sailboarding is one of the most popular activities in the gorge. Surfers migrate from all over the world to enjoy the near-perfect conditions of wind and water on the reservoir behind the Bonneville Dam, a huge lake stretching 40 miles long and more than a mile wide. Most days you'll see hundreds of athletic sailboarding enthusiasts gracefully flying over the reservoir's glistening surface under multicolored sails.

On the occasional calm day, sailboarders take advantage of other gorge activities. Many enjoy bicycling. The Gorge Challenge, a popular, moderately difficult ride, includes many of the region's highlights.

The route begins at Maryhill, a unique mansion-turned-art-museum, spectacularly located on bluffs overlooking the gorge.

The grounds include well-kept lawns and flower gardens defended by peacocks. The museum houses major collections of Auguste Rodin's sculptures and drawings, Native American art, and Romanian and Russian crafts, and attracts many traveling displays. Allow time to explore the museum and perhaps to visit the full-size Stonehenge reproduction located 4 miles away, also built by the eccentric millionaire Sam Hill.

The ride begins with a 5-mile climb up to the Klickitat plateau, a region of rolling hills 1,000 feet above the gorge. It's a challenging ascent, so you'll probably want to take breaks along the way to rest and enjoy the view of the river behind you. From the plateau you can see four major volcanic peaks: Mounts Hood, Adams, Rainier, and the recently erupted Mount St. Helens. Your first destination is the town of Goldendale, the commercial center of this farm and ranch region. If you have time, visit the Klickitat County Historical Museum, located in a Victorian mansion, for a step back in time to frontier days.

Use Mount Adams to guide your way westward through farm-covered rolling hills to the Klickitat River. The descent along the narrow river canyon is "awesome," in the words of sailboarding enthusiasts: 5 miles of winding road and beautiful scenery. The Klickitat River is one of the "usual and accustomed" sites designated for traditional dip-net fishing by members of the Klickitat Indian tribe.

You'll pass through the lumber-mill town of Klickitat and enjoy a slow and easy descent to Lyle, where the Klickitat joins the Columbia. I–84, which follows the Columbia River's Oregon side, attracts most through traffic, so Highway 14 along the Washington side has relatively light traffic. It makes this a pleasant road for bicycling. Heading east you'll enjoy being on the river side of the road for good views and usually a tailwind.

Across the river is The Dalles, the largest city on this stretch of the river. A little farther you will pass the turnoff to Horsethief Lake State Park. Many sites of prehistoric native petroglyphs were flooded with the damming of the Columbia, but dramatic examples such as "She Who Watches" remain etched on the rocks at Horsethief Park. This large, round image, a 2-mile hike from the parking lot, is surrounded by smaller stick-shaped figures, illustrating the confluence of different tribal styles. The final ride back to Maryhill is relatively flat and easy. Exploring the Columbia Gorge by bicycle, you will have tasted firsthand the power and serenity of this beautiful, windswept land.

The Basics

Start: Maryhill Museum, Hwy. 14 (the Washington side of the Columbia River), 20 miles east of The Dalles. From Portland take I–84 to Biggs, cross the river on the Maryhill Bridge, and follow signs 5 miles up the bluff.

Length: 70.9 miles.

Terrain: One major climb during the first 5 miles and several small hills farther along. Roads are generally good, with light traffic or smooth and wide shoulders.

Food: A café serves light snacks at the Maryhill Museum. There is a Ranchmart store at 3 miles; stores and restaurants in Goldendale, at 12.5 miles; in Klickitat, at 32.8 miles, and in Lyle, at 46.9 miles; and a store at 53.5 miles.

For more information: Klickitat County Visitor Center at Maryhill, P.O. Box 1220, Goldendale, WA 98620; (509) 773–4395.

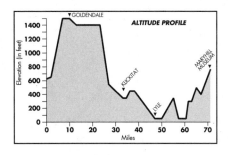

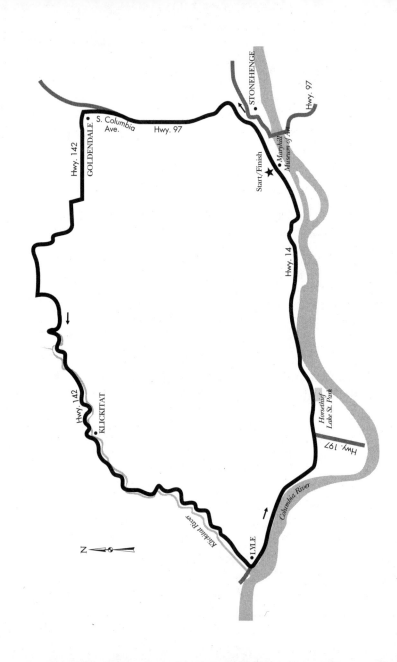

Miles & Directions

- 0.0 Turn right onto Hwy. 14 from the Maryhill Museum driveway.
- 2.4 Turn left onto Hwy. 97, which begins to climb northward up the side of the gorge.
- 9.3 Turn left onto S. Columbia Ave. (Old 97 South), which goes directly into Goldendale.
- 12.6 Turn left onto Hwy. 142 in downtown Goldendale. You will pass the Klickitat County Historical Museum to the right. Outside of Goldendale follow Mt. Adams on Hwy. 142 through a number of zigzags and down the Klickitat River Canyon.
- 32.8 Town of Klickitat. Be careful crossing angled railroad tracks in front of the Klickitat Mill.
- 46.9 Turn left onto Hwy. 14 in Lyle. Take care riding through the two tunnels just past the town.
- 54.1 Across the river is The Dalles, one of the largest cities on the Columbia. Horsethief Lake State Park turnoff is 2.0 miles farther on the right.
- 70.9 Turn right at Maryhill turnoff. End back at parking lot.

24

Yakima Wine and Fruit Challenge

Bicycling the rich farmland of the lower Yakima Valley is like riding through the Garden of Eden. As far as you can see are mild rolling hills covered with fruit trees and grapevines. This is the center of Washington State's fruit and expanding wine industries. Dan Baris of Yakima's Cascadians Bicycle Club developed this route to highlight the charms of the Yakima Valley. You will visit Prosser, Grandview, Zillah, and Sunnyside, each of which is a unique, busy, and friendly town serving its farming community. You pass by no less than sixteen wineries or tasting rooms along the way, ranging from small family businesses to major labels.

This route should delight any bicyclist who enjoys beautiful scenery, fresh fruit, wine tasting, or watching the bustle of farm life. The short, 31-mile loop, from Prosser to Grandview, is a relatively easy ride that passes seven wineries. The full route can be bicycled in two days, with a stay in Zillah, or in one hard 87-mile ride.

All of the wineries and tasting rooms listed offer tours during regular hours, although Coventry Vale, at mile 75, requests that you call ahead for an appointment. Even nondrinkers can enjoy seeing and smelling the wine-making process. Many wineries encourage visitors to tour the vineyards and enjoy a picnic lunch. For more information contact the Yakima Valley Wine Growers Association, P.O. Box 39, Grandview, WA 98930.

Prosser, the start and end point of this ride, was founded on the Yakima River in the late 1800s at the site of a natural waterfall, allowing easy construction of a water-powered gristmill. It is now the county seat and a bustling community. The local historical society museum at Patterson and Seventh is worth visiting to learn more about the community's development.

The route's first few miles follow the Yakima River, passing a winery of the same name. It's a beautiful countryside of small family farms, vineyards, and sandy, dry pastures. You'll enjoy an especially memorable view of the valley at the point where Old Inland Empire Highway curves into Old Prosser Road. Small vineyards, orchards, and vegetable farms lie spread out along the bright green river valley, contrasting with a backdrop of dry, sagebrush-covered hills.

A few miles farther you'll ride into Grandview, past the Chateau Ste. Michelle tasting room. Grandview's turn-of-the-century business district is listed on the National Register of Historic Places, as are some of the older neighborhoods. The shorter loop turns back to Prosser here. Riders continuing west on the longer ride may want to take a pleasant side trip through downtown.

For several miles the route follows Emerald Granger Road around Snipes Mountain, a surprising geological structure towering above the valley floor. From halfway up the "mountain," you'll enjoy a magnificent view of the meandering Yakima River below, with farms and hills beyond. Stewart Vineyards is farther up Snipes Mountain, on Cherry Hill Road. Savor the serenity of this hilltop retreat, because in a few miles you'll be riding to the town of Zillah on the shoulder of a busy highway.

Since you've surely worked up an appetite, you may want to stop at El Ranchito, an authentic Mexican restaurant and market on the outskirts of Zillah. At El Ranchito you can enjoy spicy food and the sound of the Spanish language in an informal atmosphere. A 9-mile loop through the orchard-covered hills above Zillah passes five wineries and, during the harvest season, several fruit stands. This route rewards both the palate and the eyes, with outstanding views of the valley stretching 50 miles east. It is ideal for bicyclists looking for a short ride.

You'll see plenty of hop farms on the stretch of ride from Zillah to Prosser. The Yakima Valley produces about three-quarters of all hops grown in the United States. They grow as vines, which are strung on a grid of wires between tall wood poles. Harvesting the flavorful hop cones, now mechanized, was once a labor-intensive process that attracted thousands of workers, many of them Indian, to field camps. Halfway back to Prosser you'll pass through downtown Sunnyside. Once an idealistic religious colony, the town is now the largest commercial center in the lower valley. Outside of town you'll pass by the Tucker Cellars tasting room and fruit market and soon return to Grandview on the Yakima Valley Highway.

The last 20 miles, through the Roza district along the northeast edge of the valley, are some of the most enjoyable. There are vineyards and small orchards almost as far as the eye can see. You'll pass three small wineries, then descend back into Prosser. It's a 2-mile side trip east of town to visit the last two wineries. You'll want to bring your panniers for this ride to carry the numerous samples you'll enjoy collecting.

The Basics

Start: Sixth Ave. and Meade Ave. in downtown Prosser. Take exit 80 off I–82, and follow signs 1.5 miles. Continue straight after crossing the Yakima River into downtown.

Length: 31 or 87 miles. The 9-mile loop north of Zillah can also be enjoyed as a separate ride.

Terrain: Flat to rolling hills with a few longer climbs. Mostly low-traffic rural roads and a few stretches of busy highway with good shoulders.

Food: Stores and restaurants in Prosser; Grandview, at 10.5 miles; Zillah, at 36.5 miles; Sunnyside, at 62 miles; and Grandview at 68.5 miles. There is a small store at 19.4 miles. Wineries listed typically offer wine tasting and light snacks. Fruit and vegetable stands available seasonally.

For more information: Zillah Chamber of Commerce, P.O. Box 1294, Zillah, WA 98953; (509) 829–5055.

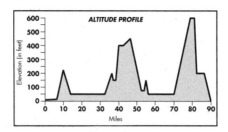

Miles & Directions

- 0.0 Head north on 6th Ave. In 4 blocks bear left at stop sign intersection to continue north on the Wine Country Hwy., across the Yakima River.
- 0.5 Immediately after crossing the river, turn left onto N. River Rd.
- 1.2 Turn left to stay on N. River Rd. Stay on this road for the next 2.5 miles as it follows the Yakima River.
- 3.6 Turn right onto Wilgus Rd.
- 4.5 Turn left onto Old Inland Empire Hwy.
- 7.2 Road curves right, becomes Old Prosser Rd. As it curves you'll enjoy a beautiful view of the valley below.
- 9.5 Bear left onto 5th St. at bottom of small hill, as you approach the town of Grandview.
- 10.2 Follow road as it curves left at intersection with Division St. Continue west on 5th St. In 2.0 miles it becomes Grandview Pavement Rd., with 3.0 miles of rough concrete surface.

For the short loop, turn right (north) on Division St. where it intersects with 5th and go through downtown Grandview. In 0.5 mile turn right at stop sign onto E. Main Street/Wine Country Hwy. In 1.0 mile turn left onto McCreadie Rd., cross I–82, and continue following instructions at mile 70.8.

- 15.0 Turn right onto Mabton-Sunnyside Rd.
- 15.5 Turn left onto Green Valley Rd.

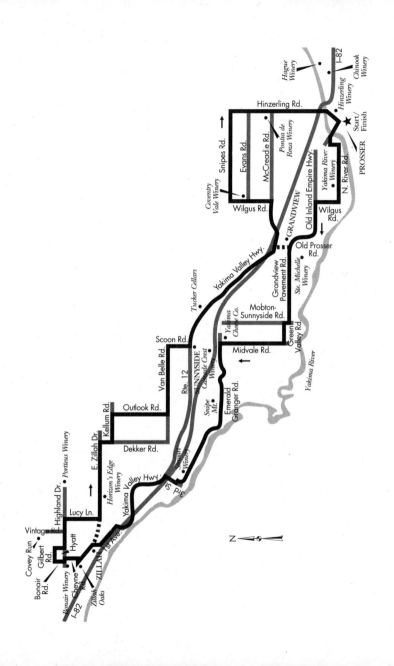

- 16.5 Turn right onto Midvale Rd.
- 19.4 Turn left onto Emerald Granger Rd.
- 21.5 Turn right at T intersection to stay on Emerald Granger Rd. Be careful crossing angled railroad tracks in 1.0 mile.
- 26.5 Follow road as it curves left at the top of a small climb.
- 28.9 Turn left then immediate right onto 3rd St. This crosses over railroad tracks and under I–82.
- 29.6 Turn left onto the Yakima Valley Hwy.
- 34.4 Pass Teapot gas station, listed on the National Register of Historic Places.
- 35.0 Cross over I–82 (twice), then turn left onto 1st Ave.
- 36.3 Pass through downtown Zillah. Be careful riding over angled railroad tracks outside of town.

The next 9 miles, which passes by five wineries, can be enjoyed as a separate loop. To return to downtown Zillah, turn right onto E. Zillah Dr. from Lucy Lane at mile 46.5.

- 36.7 Turn right onto Cheyne Rd.
- 38.5 Turn left onto Highland Dr.
- 39.5 Turn right onto Bonair Rd.
- 40.5 Turn right onto Gilbert Rd.
- 42.0 Turn right onto Roza Dr.
- 43.0 Turn left onto Highland Dr.
- 44.5 Turn right onto Lucy Ln.
- 46.5 Turn left onto E. Zillah Dr. (or right to return to downtown Zillah).
- 51.5 Turn right at stop sign onto Dekker Rd.
- 52.5 Turn left on Kellum Rd.
- 54.0 Turn right at stop sign onto Outlook Rd.
- 57.0 Turn left onto Van Belle Rd.
- 60.4 Turn right onto Scoon Rd.
- 61.4 Cross the Yakima Valley Hwy., and several sets of railroad tracks, into the town of Sunnyside. Follow the road as it curves left, becoming Zillah Rd.
- 62.0 Turn left onto Edison through downtown Sunnyside.
- 63.2 Turn right onto the Yakima Valley Hwy. Optional gravel

path parallels highway for several miles.

- 68.3 Cross under I–82, and continue through town of Grand-view.
- 70.8 Turn left onto McCreadie Rd., crossing over I–82.
- 73.3 Turn left onto Wilgus Rd.
- 76.4 Turn right onto Snipes Rd.
- 79.4 Turn right onto Hinzerling Rd.
- 85.6 Cross over I–82, then the Yakima River. Turn left onto 10th Ave. In 2 blocks bear left onto the Wine Country Hwy.
- 86.3 Turn right onto Meade Ave.
- 87.0 End back in downtown Prosser.

25

North Wheatland Cruise

Walla Walla—Waitsburg—Walla Walla

Cayuse Indians have long inhabited the Walla Walla Valley, which they called "The Place of the People of the Rye Grass." Located between the Palouse region of mild rolling hills, to the north, and the Blue Mountain, to the south and east, this region is still known primarily for fertile fields of grain, now wheat. Rolling hills covered with huge farms (one thousand acres are common), as well as hospitable towns, make this region attractive for bicycling.

Walla Walla is an ideal base for bicycle trips. Members of the Wheatland Wheelers bicycling club jokingly call the local roads "20-foot paved bike paths" because of their extremely low traffic. The city, starting as a fort in 1856, has long provided commercial, educational, and social services to the region. You'll enjoy the quiet downtown, which retains many turn-of-the-century buildings, pleasant neighborhood streets lined with arching old trees, and the distinguished Whitman College campus. Be sure to visit the Whitman Mission site, now a national park, 7 miles west of town.

Most of the farms here are in dry-land winter wheat, which means that farmers plant their crops in the fall and rely on natural precipitation for irrigation. Autumn rains give the wheat a healthy start. It overwinters as short green plants, which help control erosion. Of course, farming without irrigation is a gamble—a drought year means crop failure.

Although crops cover most of the land, you can still find

plenty of wildlife living around creek beds, steep hillsides, and roadside ditches. Watch for hawks, magpies (a relative of the crow, with blue-and-white wings and long tail feathers), and grouse, which locals call "prairie chickens."

The following two routes are typical of the club's offerings; each is a delightful adventure, and together they form a sanctioned century.

The North Wheatland Cruise goes through downtown Walla Walla, then north along Dry Creek and over wheat-field-covered hills to Waitsburg. Waitsburg is a friendly town devoted to supplying the needs of local farmers and bicyclists. It was founded in 1871 adjacent to the Touchet River, which provided power for a large grain mill. The four-story mill still stands, and its original millstone can be seen in Coppei Park, 1 block to your left as you enter town. The town retains much of its nineteenth-century character.

Grain elevators and clusters of well-kept farm buildings that dot the countryside demonstrate the industriousness of local farmers. You can learn a lot about a farm by its grain storage. Early in the twentieth century, bulk storage was built of wood planks, with 2 x 10s laid flat at the lowest level and tapering to 2 x 8s and 2 x 6s higher up where pressures are less. These elevators reached as high as 50 feet. Many still stand along railroad tracks, now usually covered with corrugated metal. Later taller grain elevators were built of poured cement. After World War II, trucking replaced much railroad shipping, reducing the need for large centralized storage. Many farms now have metal storage bins, and

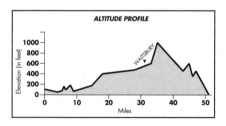

138

sometimes farmers will simply store excess wheat temporarily on the ground under sheets of plastic.

Eat, drink, and rest at Waitsburg, because the first few miles out of town involve a 500-foot climb. At the top you will be rewarded with a magnificent view of the farmlands and rolling hills that surround Walla Walla, as well as the Blue Mountains to the southeast. From there it's an easy ride back to Walla Walla over mild rolling hills.

The Basics

Start: Begin at Park St. and Boyer Ave. on the west side of the Whitman College campus. From Hwy. 12 head south on 2nd Ave. in downtown Walla Walla, turn left on Main St. and right on Park.

Length: 24.2 or 50.8 miles.

Terrain: Good roads over flat to rolling hills. Moderate climbs approaching and leaving Waitsburg.

Food: Restaurants and stores in Waitsburg, at 33 miles.

For more information: Wheatland Wheelers Bike Club, P.O. Box 2315, Walla Walla, WA 99362.

Miles & Directions

- 0.0 Go north on Park St. 2 blocks, then left on Rose St.
- 1.1 Right on 9th Ave. (Mullan).
- 1.4 Turn left on Pine St., then turn right on 13th Ave. Go under Hwy. 12.
- 1.9 Turn left on Dell Ave., which parallels Hwy. 12.
- 3.5 Follow Dell Ave. as it curves left, then take the first right turn on Baldwin Rd.
- 4.3 Bear right at intersection on Sudbury Rd. Climb a small hill, and then descend into open farmland.
- 9.2 Cross Dry Creek, then turn right on Loney Rd., just before a cluster of grain elevators.

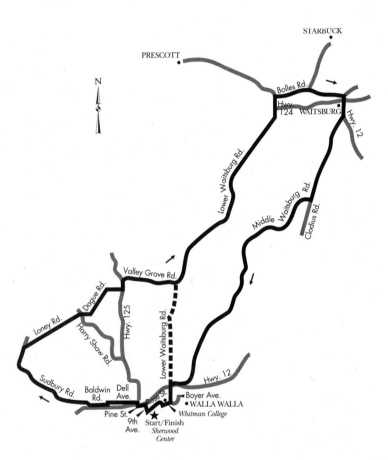

STARBUCK

PRESCOTT

N

Bolles Rd.

Hwy. 124   WAITSBURG

Hwy. 12

Lower Waitsburg Rd.

Middle Waitsburg Rd.

Clodius Rd.

Valley Grove Rd.

Dague Rd.

Loney Rd.

Hwy. 125

Harry Shaw Rd.

Lower Waitsburg Rd.

Hwy. 12

Sudbury Rd.

Baldwin Rd.

Dell Ave.

Rose St.

Boyer Ave.
● WALLA WALLA

Whitman College

Pine St.

9th Ave.

Start/Finish
Sherwood Center

- 12.2 Turn right on Harvey Shaw Rd.
- 12.3 Turn left on Dague Rd., after crossing Dry Creek.
- 14.9 Turn left onto Hwy. 125.
- 15.2 Continue straight where the highway curves left, onto Valley Grove Rd. Ride under the trestle, and follow the railroad line.

For the 24.2-mile option—

Turn right at 18.0 miles onto Lower Waitsburg Rd. Cross Hwy. 12 at 23.1 miles; road becomes Clinton St. Turn right onto Boyer Ave. at 23.7 miles, and end back at Park Street.

- 18.0 Turn left onto Lower Waitsburg Rd. Here you will encounter one of the two major climbs of this ride. Fortunately halfway up there is a small clump of trees for a shady rest.
- 27.8 Turn left on Hwy. 124, toward Prescott. This is part of the official Lewis and Clark Trail.
- 28.8 Take the first right turn onto Bolles Rd. just after crossing the Touchet River. Be careful riding over angled railroad tracks.
- 30.3 Continue straight onto Menoken Rd., bypassing the turnoff to Starbuck.
- 32.0 Follow the road as it curves right and crosses the Touchet River again. This becomes Main St. in downtown Waitsburg. You can take the first left to Coppei Park, or go straight into downtown.
- 32.1 Turn left onto Hwy. 124, and a block farther turn right onto Hwy. 12 (Coppei Ave.) west toward Walla Walla.
- 33.0 Turn right onto Middle Waitsburg Rd. You will have a 1.8-mile climb.
- 49.7 Turn left onto Lower Waitsburg Rd. Take care crossing Hwy. 12, as well as the railroad tracks at the bottom of a short descent just past the highway.
- 50.3 Turn right onto Boyer Ave.
- 50.8 End back at Park St.

26

Blue Mountain Cruise

Walla Walla—Milton Freewater
Weston—Barrett—Walla Walla

When pioneers crossed the Blue Mountains into what is now Washington, they faced one of the last major challenges of their journey west. Having walked more than 1,000 miles of dirt roads and rough mountain trails, the settlers found rest and care at Whitman Mission in the Walla Walla Valley. The fertile valley, then being tilled by white farmers for the first time, must have looked awfully pleasant after months of difficult travel. Now the valley is filled with lush orchards, and wheat farms cover the surrounding hills.

This loop, used by the Wheatland Wheelers as a half-century ride, begins on the campus of Whitman College. It goes through the residential neighborhoods and semirural lands south of town, then descends into the lower farm- and orchard lands along the Walla Walla Valley, crossing the Oregon border toward the town of Milton Freewater.

When they use this route for their organized events, the Wheatland Wheelers provide a food and rest stop in Milton Freewater. You may want to stop for a snack and perhaps visit the Fraiser Homestead Pioneer Museum to learn about the lives of local settlers. Leaving town you'll face a 2-mile climb and then a 1-mile descent to cool off. Turn right at the bottom of the hill for the shorter 36-mile route, or continue south along Dry Creek Road and up the 2-mile climb over the wheat-covered hills to the charming old town of Weston, off Highway 204.

After you've explored Weston's historic downtown, which consists of two cafés, a barber shop, and a bank–turned–city hall, you'll be ready for the relatively easy ride on Highway 11 back to Dry Creek Road, and then the enjoyable descent through the narrow canyon toward Barrett.

Barrett is nothing more than a railroad siding and grain elevator, located where the canyon opens into a flat valley of orchards and small ranches. A few miles farther you'll cross the border back into Washington. The ride is flat until the final 5 miles; there's a last hill with an enjoyable view of the area you just passed. You'll ride through College Place, a small town that developed around Walla Walla College and back through downtown Walla Walla to end at Whitman College.

The Basics

Start: Begin at Park St. and Boyer Ave. on the west side of the Whitman College campus. From Hwy. 12 head south on 2nd Ave. in downtown Walla Walla; turn left on Main St. and right on Park St.
Length: 36 or 49 miles.
Terrain: Good roads over flat to major hills. The biggest hill is on the longer option, approaching Weston.
Food: Restaurants and stores in Milton Freewater, at 12 miles, and Weston, at 22.7 miles.
For more information: Walla Walla Chamber of Commerce, Sumach and Colville, Walla Walla, WA 99362; (509) 525–0850.

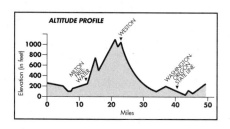

WALLA WALLA

Whitman College
Start/Finish

Rose St.

COLLEGE PLACE

Walla Walla College

Park St.

Howard St.

Hwy. 125

Prospect Ave.

Mojonnier Rd.

College Ave.

Dalles Military Rd.

Puppers Rd.

Beet Rd.

WASHINGTON

OREGON

State Line

Tum-A-Lum Rd.

Birch Creek Rd.

Eastside Rd.

Winesap Rd.

N

N. Elizabeth St.

MILTON FREEWATER

Fraiser Homestead Museum

Dry Creek Rd.

Barrett

Winn Rd.

Hwy. 11

Hwy. 204

WESTON

Water St.

Miles & Directions

- 0.0 Head south on Park St.
- 0.8 Bear right, onto Howard St. You'll ride past Howard Tietan Park, to the left, and the old Mountain View Cemetery to the right.
- 2.2 Turn right at the four-way stop sign onto Prospect Ave. Zigzag left and right at 3rd Ave. and at Taumarson Rd. to continue west on Prospect.
- 5.0 Continue straight at the stop sign onto Dalles Military Rd. Follow the road as it zigzags and becomes Puppers Rd.
- 7.0 After crossing the Walla Walla River, turn left onto State Line Rd., at the top of a small ridge. This immediately curves right to become Tum-A-Lum Rd.
- 8.8 Turn left on Birch Creek Rd. After crossing Birch Creek the road curves right, then forks. Bear right onto Eastside Rd., toward Milton Freewater.
- 10.4 Stay on Eastside Rd. as it curves right.
- 11.4 Cross Grouse Creek and Hwy. 11, then turn left onto N. Elizabeth St.
- 12.3 Turn left onto Main St., which is also Hwy. 11, through Milton Freewater.
- 13.3 Bear right to stay on Hwy. 11 (or take a detour 3 blocks to the left to visit the Fraiser Homestead Pioneer Museum), and begin the 2-mile climb out of town.
- 14.0 Turn right onto Dry Creek Rd., and continue climbing for another mile. From the top you'll be rewarded with a panoramic view that stretches back to Walla Walla and the Palouse hills beyond. You'll enjoy a cooling descent for the next mile.

For the short option turn right toward Barrett at 16.0 miles and continue as described at mile 29.0.

- 19.4 Cross Hwy. 11 onto Winn Rd. Begin a 2-mile climb.
- 21.6 Continue straight onto Hwy. 204, toward Weston.
- 21.8 Bear left at fork, toward Weston.

- 22.2 Bear left onto Water St., south into Weston.
- 22.7 Turn around in downtown Weston.
- 23.2 Continue straight on Water St., which becomes Hwy. 204 west.
- 24.0 Turn right onto Hwy. 11.
- 26.5 Turn left onto Dry Creek Rd.
- 29.0 Turn left toward Barrett. Enjoy the descent through this pleasant narrow valley, but be careful riding over angled railroad tracks.
- 34.3 Turn right toward Milton Freewater.
- 36.2 Turn left onto Winesap Rd.
- 40.2 Turn right onto State Line Rd., then take the immediate left onto Beet Rd.
- 41.2 Bear left at fork to stay on Beet Rd.
- 42.2 Bear right onto Mojonnier Rd. Cross bridge over Walla Walla River, then follow Mojonnier Rd. as it zigzags up a small hill over the valley.
- 44.4 Turn left onto College Ave., an urban arterial, past Walla Walla College.
- 45.7 Bear right at fork onto Rose St. toward downtown Walla Walla.
- 48.8 Turn right on Park St.
- 49.0 End at Boyer Ave.

27

Williams Lake Cruise

Spokane—Cheney—Turnbull Wildlife Refuge
Williams Lake—Cheney—Spokane

This route from Spokane to Cheney and Williams Lake is a favorite Saturday ride for Spokane Bicycle Club members. It's a perfect way to explore the communities, farms, and wildlands in southwest Spokane County. The Williams Lake Resort café at the halfway point is a popular lunch stop.

The route starts at the Coeur d'Alene Park in Spokane's historic Browne's Addition, a neighborhood with many beautiful nineteenth-century homes. The ride begins with a short but fast descent on Inland Empire Way, then follows a series of rural roads away from the city and up to the plateau of small farms and rolling hills south of Spokane.

The route goes through downtown Cheney, home of Eastern Washington University and a commercial center for area farmers. If you are already hungry, there are plenty of places to eat. Outside of town on the Cheney-Plaza Road, you'll ride several miles through the heart of the Turnbull National Wildlife Refuge. The light automobile traffic on this road allows bicyclists to enjoy the ponderosa pine forest's subtle beauty and view the abundant wildlife. During spring and early summer, the refuge's lush marshes and ponds provide food for wild ducks, swans, and passing animals.

A few miles past the refuge, you'll turn onto Williams Lake Road and soon arrive at the resort. The resort's café offers hearty lunches, and if you like you can rent a boat for exploring the lake. A few miles farther the route turns onto Mullinix Road, another low-traffic road through ranch lands and scattered forests, back to Cheney. From there you can choose between the fast, direct Cheney-Spokane Road or slower but more pleasant secondary farm roads. Betz Road, which meanders over rolling, grain-covered hills, is an especially beautiful ride. The route then zigzags on rural roads back to Spokane, taking the Sunset Boulevard Bridge over Latah Creek and back to Coeur d'Alene Park.

The Basics

Start: Coeur d'Alene Park, at 4th Ave. and Spruce St. in the Browne's Addition. From downtown Spokane, take 2nd Ave. west. Continue 4 blocks past Sunset Blvd.

Length: 68 miles, 38 miles (Spokane to Cheney), or 30 miles (Cheney to Williams Lake).

Terrain: Mostly rural riding over rolling hills, with one major climb early in the ride.

Food: Stores and restaurants in Cheney at 16 and 45 miles; Williams Lake Resort Café, at 31.5 miles; convenience store at 54.7 miles.

For more information: Cheney Chamber of Commerce, P.O. Box 65, Cheney, WA 99004; (509) 235–8480.

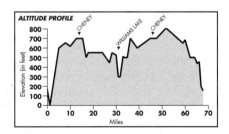

Miles & Directions

- 0.0 Ride east on 4th Ave.
- 0.2 Turn right on Cannon St., then an immediate right onto Sunset Blvd. Merge into the center lane onto Inland Empire Way, toward Pulman and Colfax.
- 1.5 Turn right on 23rd Ave., bear left on Chestnut, then right on Thorpe Rd.
- 1.8 Cross Hwy. 195, and pass under two railroad trestles.
- 3.6 Turn left at stop sign on Assembly Rd.
- 5.4 Turn right on Hallett Rd.
- 7.5 Turn left on Spotted Rd.
- 9.7 Turn right on Andrus Rd.
- 14.4 Turn right on the Cheney-Spokane Rd.
- 15.5 Turn left on 1st St., which is also Hwy. 904. Ride through downtown Cheney.
- 16.8 Turn left opposite K St. onto Cheney-Plaza Rd.
- 21.0 Turnbull Wildlife Refuge headquarters.
- 28.1 Turn right on Williams Lake Rd.
- 31.5 Williams Lake Resort.
- 32.8 Turn right onto Mullinix Rd.
- 44.1 Turn right onto Hwy. 904.
- 46.0 Pass through downtown Cheney.

For a direct route back to Spokane, turn right on Cheney-Spokane Rd.

- 47.5 Just outside of Cheney, cross carefully over angled railroad tracks, then turn left on Betz Rd.
- 48.4 Turn right to stay on Betz Rd.
- 52.0 Turn right onto Granite Lake Rd.
- 54.1 Turn right on Medical Lake Rd.
- 54.5 Turn left on Hwy. 904. In 0.2 mile, turn right, just past the Exxon station, onto Melville Rd.
- 58.8 Turn left on Spotted Rd.
- 60.3 Turn right on Hallett Rd.
- 62.3 Turn left on Assembly Rd.
- 65.0 Turn right on Garden Springs Rd.

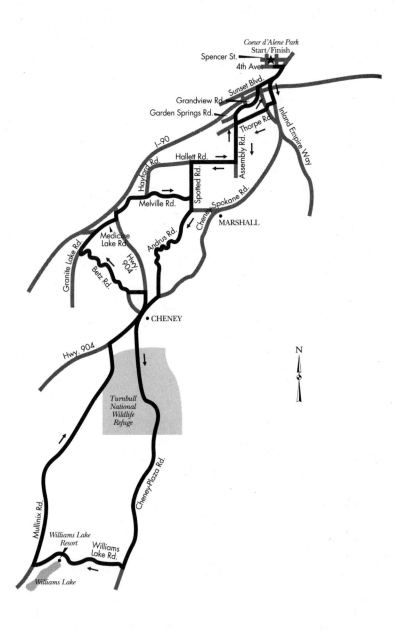

- 65.4 Turn right on Grandview Rd.
- 65.8 Follow road as it curves right, then take the immediate left onto 16th Ave. for a steep descent.
- 66.4 Turn left on Milton Rd., right on 14th Ave., then left onto Lindeke St. Cross bridge over I–90.
- 67.0 Turn right onto Sunset Blvd. Cross high bridge over Latah Creek.
- 67.6 Turn left on Cannon and an immediate left on 4th Ave.
- 68.0 End back at Coeur d'Alene Park.

28

Centennial Trail Ramble

Riverfront Park—Boulder Beach—Riverfront Park

Spokane's Centennial Trail is one of the most enjoyable of the rails-to-trails projects in the Pacific Northwest. It follows the Spokane River through the city, linking parks, historical sites, and urban attractions to form a unique green-space corridor. Highlights include the Little Spokane River natural area, Riverfront Park, Spokane Falls, Gonzaga University campus, and beautiful geological formations around Mirabeau Park. The 37-mile trail goes from Nine Mile Dam, west of Spokane, to the Idaho border. There it connects with the 23-mile North Idaho Centennial Trail. If you have the energy, you can ride all of the way to Idaho's beautiful Lake Coeur d'Alene, a 73-mile round-trip. The trail consists primarily of paths, with some on-street bicycle lanes.

The Centennial Trail is maintained by the Washington State Parks and Recreation Commission in cooperation with the City of Spokane, the Spokane County Parks Department, and the Friends of the Centennial Trail, a citizen's group that coordinates public support for this unique facility. Over 2,500 people each "bought" a foot of the trail at the outset to help fund the project. Community groups, from the Valley Rotary to the Spokane Mountaineers, have each adopted their own mile to care for. The trail continues to grow in popularity. You can expect to share it with pedestrians, in-line skaters, joggers, power walkers, fellow recreational cyclists, and, on weekdays, a growing number of bicycle commuters.

The trail follows a route of historic and geological significance along the Spokane River. People have inhabited this location for over ten thousand years. The Coeur d'Alene, Spokane, and Colville first nations harvested salmon at Spokane Falls and enjoyed the fruits of the river valley for millennia. A fur trading post was established in the early nineteenth century, and the community expanded as more settlers arrived. The first commercial ferry in Washington Territory crossed the river near the present trail as part of the Mullan Road, which connected the Missouri and Columbia rivers. A sawmill was built there in 1871, and the city really began to grow after becoming a major railroad center over the following decade. You'll see remnants of these activities as you ride.

The ride described here follows the trail from Riverfront Park, in downtown, to Boulder Beach viewpoint, at the city's edge. The one hundred-acre Riverfront Park is a legacy of Expo 74, the environmental world's fair that helped Spokane rediscover its riverside heritage. Riverfront is a beautiful park with activities for everybody; it includes an opera house and outdoor theater. If you want to ride something that doesn't require pedaling, you can try the 1909 hand-carved Looff Carousel or take a trip on a miniature railroad. Leaving the park, you'll experience a hint of Europe as you pedal under arched trees and past strolling pedestrians. The well-tended landscape surrounding Gonzaga University gives few reminders that this area was once an industrial wasteland. Look out for fish-catching osprey, pudgy marmots, and busy warblers among the cottonwoods, willows, and tall grasses that grace the river's edge. You may even catch site of daring souls scaling the cliffs at Minnehaha Rocks across Upriver Drive. By the time you're done with your ride, you'll be convinced how precious this green corridor is for city-weary humans as well as wildlife.

The ride from Boulder Beach to the Idaho border has few human-made attractions. Interstate 90 parallels the river, but you'd never know it when bicycling much of this route. You'll relish the drama of Flora Rapids, where the river flows undammed over boulders as it has for eons. Enjoy the aroma of ancient ponderosa pines and the soft music of birdsong undisturbed by motor vehicle traffic noise. At the border you can turn around at the State Visitor Information Center, or cross the Spokane River on a separate bridge to the Idaho Centennial Trail for a 13.5-mile ride to Coeur d'Alene.

The trail is well marked and under continual development. A map is available from Friends of the Centennial Trail, P.O. Box 351, Spokane, WA 99210–0351; phone (509) 624–7188, fax (509) 624–7038. Mileage markers on the trail indicate distance from the Idaho border.

The Basics

Start: Riverfront Park in downtown Spokane. Take exit 280B from I–90, proceed north to Main St., then east to Wall St., then west (left) at Spokane Falls Blvd. to the Park. There are parking and trolley shuttle bus service available at the Spokane Arena, north of the park.

Length: 14 miles round-trip to Boulder Beach viewpoint. Longer options include 46 miles round-trip to the Idaho border and 73 miles all the way to the city of Coeur d'Alene and back.

Terrain: Mostly flat.

Food: There are no food concessions on the trail, so bring snacks and drinks.

For more information: Spokane Visitors Information, W. 926 Sprague Ave., Spokane 99204; (800) 248–3230 or (509) 747–3230. Riverside State Park, (509) 456–2729 or 456–3964.

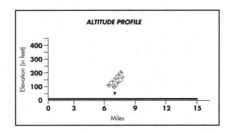

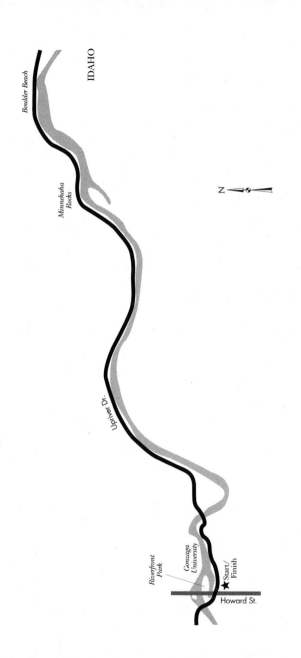

IDAHO

Boulder Beach

Minnehaha
Rocks

Upriver Dr.

Riverfront
Park

Gonzaga
University

★ Start/
Finish

Howard St.

N

Miles & Directions

- 0.0 Ride south along the riverbank through the park, and follow it east past the playground, opera house, and agricultural trade center.
- 1.0 Follow the trail over Don Kardong Bridge to Gonzaga University, and continue east on overpass to Mission Park.
- 2.0 Cross Mission St. and proceed east (right) on sidewalk. Cross Upriver Dr. to east side and proceed north on bicycle lane.
- 6.0 Turn right and follow Upriver Dr. along the river to Boulder Beach viewpoint.
- 7.0 Turn around. Return as you came on bicycle lanes, or follow the narrower riverside trail. Be cautious and courteous of other trail users if you take this route.
- 14.0 End at Riverfront Park.

29

Spokane Autumn Century Classic

Spokane—Deer Park—Blanchard Pass
Spirit Lake—Rathdrum—Argonne Hill

What's required to produce a major bicycling event? A lot of enthusiasm, work, and fun, to start. Mix in publicity, maps, and food. You'll need good roads, enjoyable scenery, and perhaps some major climbs to challenge participants. Finally, add bicyclists, and a dash of good weather, and you've got a pleasing, satisfying, and successful century ride. The Spokane, Washington, Autumn Century, held in mid-September, is an excellent example of this recipe.

Over the years the Spokane club has developed the skills and resources to manage effective bicycle events. They use several well-mapped courses, marked with "Dan Henry" arrows painted at each intersection. A pool of volunteers takes on various tasks: Some organize publicity and registration, others take responsibility for food preparation and rest stops. Local bicycle shops provide emergency patrols, bicycle-mounted radio operators maintain communication.

Cases of bananas, hundreds of cookies, dozens of sandwiches, and gallons of drinks are assembled the morning of the ride. Tables are set up early, with information packets readied for each participant so the 350 bicyclists can be registered quickly. The bicyclists soon scatter around the various courses. Since bicyclists are always moving, the food needs to keep pace, progressing from one rest stop to another, and the communication network must be constantly roving.

Midafternoon the fastest riders return. These are the hotshot racers. They get a big congratulations for their fast times. As the afternoon progresses more riders return, smiling with pride or sometimes wincing with pain. The last riders arrive by early evening. Event organizers must sometimes rescue a few lost participants. Then it's time to pack and clean up.

Is it worth it? The members of the Spokane Bicycle Club find that their volunteer efforts are repaid many times over with years of pleasurable riding, friendship, and the knowledge that they contribute to making an event like the Autumn Century safe and enjoyable to all participants. Next time you join in an organized club event, be sure to thank the volunteers for their efforts.

Although Spokane is the second-largest city in Washington State, it still has a frontier spirit. It's in a beautiful region of homestead farms and pine forest–covered hills surrounded by mountains. The Spokane Autumn Century Challenge is an ideal way to explore this striking countryside with support from the enthusiastic Spokane Bicycle Club.

The ride starts at the north end of Spokane. A quick ride along Shep Creek and Dartford Canyon takes you to the Wild Rose Prairie, one of several rich farming areas you'll enjoy during this ride. You soon pass through the small agricultural town of Deer Park, then head east, first through the narrow Little Spokane River Valley, and then over Blanchard Pass. Blanchard is only 2,442 feet, low as mountain passes go. But if you are not accustomed to mountain riding, it can be quite a challenge. It begins with a mild, steady climb at Reflection Lake. Three miles from the summit the climbing becomes steeper, about a 5 percent grade. The last mile is a challenging 7 percent pull.

Can you do it? Taking this challenge is the only way to find out. Make sure that you eat and drink during the approach because you'll need the energy. Climb slow and steady in low gear. Rest as often as you need. You may even decide to walk for short stretches; it will feel good to use different muscles, and walking is good exercise, too! At the summit the club provides a food stop, where riders recover and share the pleasure of their achievement.

Your ascent to Blanchard Pass is rewarded with a beautiful descent across the Idaho border. You're surrounded by forests, rolling hills, and small ranches. You may want to visit the old business district of Spirit Lake, where Maggie's Missouri Mule Restaurant proudly proclaims "Our service is lousy, but boy are we friendly," and the Whitehorse Saloon is little changed since the town was founded in 1907.

Continue through the flat Rathdrum Prairie and back across the border to Washington. The club provides a much-appreciated final rest and food stop at the historic Plante Ferry Park. You ride through the suburban communities of Trentwood and Pasadena Park, then make the last climb over Argonne Hill to the wheat fields of the Peone Prairie. From there it's an easy ride through the town of Mead and back to your starting point at the Wandermere Mall.

The Basics

Start: Wandermere Mall at the corner of N. Division St. and Hastings Rd., about 5 miles north of downtown Spokane. Note: Bicycling is not allowed on Division St. Choose another route if you arrive by bicycle.

Length: 98.2 miles.

Terrain: Alternate rolling hills and flat valleys, with a major climb over Blanchard Pass. Roads are primarily in good shape, although some in Idaho have narrow shoulders.

Food: Stores and restaurants in Deer Park, at 18.5 miles; store at intersection of Deer Park–Milan Rd. and Hwy. 2 at 25.1 miles; stores in Blanchard, at 46.2 miles; Spirit Lake, at 54 miles; Rathdrum, at 66 miles; Hauser Lake, at 73.2; Newman Lake, at 76.5; and in the town of Mead, at 95.3 miles.

For more information: Spokane Bicycle Club, P.O. Box 62, Spokane, WA 99210.

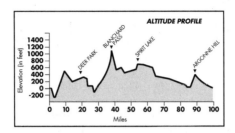

Miles & Directions

- 0.0 Head west on Hastings Rd. at the south end of Wandermere Mall. Cross Division at the traffic light.
- 1.0 Turn right onto Mill Rd.
- 2.4 Acute left at stop sign onto Dartford Rd. at the bottom of hill.
- 6.5 Left onto Monroe Rd. Follow the road as it curves.
- 11.0 Turn right at the Wild Rose Cemetery to stay on Monroe Rd.
- 18.1 Cross Hwy. 395. Road becomes Crawford St. as you ride through the town of Deer Park.
- 20.2 Road is now called Deer Park–Milan Rd.
- 25.1 Cross Hwy. 2. Store and restaurant at intersection. Continue on Deer Park–Milan Rd. downhill.
- 26.0 Turn left onto Milan-Elk Rd., just after you cross the Little Spokane River.
- 27.0 Bear right to stay on Milan-Elk Rd.
- 30.0 Turn right at stop sign on Elk-Chattaroy Rd.
- 31.6 Follow Elk-Chattaroy Rd. as it curves right, then turn left in 0.5 mile onto Blanchard Rd. Work your way up to Blanchard Pass.
- 38.0 Top of pass. Check your brakes for the coming descent.
- 43.4 State line; cross into Idaho.
- 46.2 Turn right at T onto Idaho Hwy. 41. E-Z Stop store at the junction.
- 54.0 Pass through the town of Spirit Lake. You will find mod-

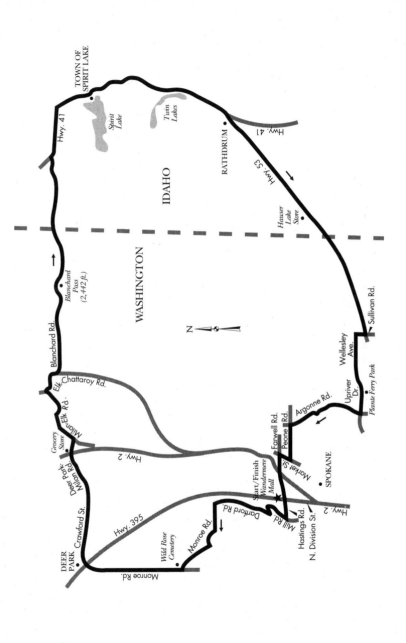

ern food stores along the highway. One block to the right on Maine St. are a number of fun old businesses in the historic downtown.

- 65.2 Enter the town of Rathdrum. Continue straight onto Hwy. 53 through downtown. You'll find restaurants and stores, as well as a nice park at the far side of town. Continue west on Hwy. 53.
- 73.2 Hauser Lake store.
- 75.0 Cross back into Washington State. Hwy. 53 becomes Hwy. 290.
- 83.0 Turn off of the highway at the Sullivan Rd. exit. Turn right, heading north on Sullivan.
- 83.3 Turn left at stop sign onto Wellesley Ave. Follow the road as it becomes Upriver Dr. along the Spokane River.
- 85.3 Plante Ferry Park.
- 87.5 Turn right at stop sign on Argonne Rd.
- 89.0 Top of Argonne hill.
- 92.2 Argonne Rd. becomes Bruce Rd.
- 92.8 Turn left onto Peone Rd.
- 95.1 Take care crossing railroad tracks!
- 95.3 Turn right on Market St. in the town of Mead.
- 95.8 Turn left onto Farwell Rd.
- 97.0 Cross Hwy. 2 at light, then bear left in 0.5 mile onto Hastings Rd.
- 98.2 End back at Wandermere Mall.

30

Pend Oreille Cruise

Ione—Sullivan Lake
Metaline Falls—Ione—Newport

Much of the Northwest landscape was sculpted into its current shape by the last ice age. Glaciers moving south formed Puget Sound and the Strait of Georgia in the west and carved huge canyons (called coulees) through eastern Washington, Idaho, and British Columbia. Bright blue lakes filled these canyons when the glaciers receded. Slowly, layers of silt turned the lakes into flat and fertile river valleys surrounded by green forested hills. The Pend Oreille (Pahn-do-ray) River Valley, which crosses the northeast corner of Washington State, is a typical example.

This route, which is part of a series of bicycle tours called Ride Around Washington, can be enjoyed either as a loop to Sullivan Lake or an overnight trip through the Pend Oreille River Valley to the town of Newport at the Idaho border. Since most automobile traffic through the valley follows the river's west bank on Highway 20, Le Clerc Road on the east bank is excellent for bicycling. You have the road to yourself for most of the trip, surrounded by the sparkling river, mountains, green forests, and fertile fields. A day of riding along the Pend Oreille River is a day of pleasure.

The river has a colorful history. This region has long been settled by Native Americans, whom explorers named Pend Oreille, French vernacular for "earrings," despite the fact that local tribes did not wear such ornaments. During the frontier days of the late nineteenth century, the Pend Oreille River served as a major transportation corridor. A small fleet of steamships plied the river, providing access to small communities before railroads or highways developed. Ione (Ehy-ohn), the ride's starting point, is a small town that once had the largest lumber mill in northeast Washington.

The first 5 miles, to Sullivan Lake, is the only significant climb of this ride. The lake is situated in a low spot between Sand Creek Mountain and Hall Mountain. After ascending 800 feet you coast down to the lake, follow the lakeshore, then coast farther down to the town of Mataline Falls. From there follow Highway 31 south along the Pend Oreille River back to Ione.

Before riding south to Newport, be sure to stock up on supplies; the route along the river's east bank has few services. Watch for the herds of buffalo that are raised for meat on the Kalispel Indian Reservation. This is the smallest Indian reservation in the United States. In Indian language, Kalispel means "eater of Camas," a beautiful blue flower that grows in wet areas throughout the valley; its root bulb was an important food for local native people. Halfway through the reservation you'll pass the Manresa Grotto, a natural cave (with a stone altar) that has been used for Catholic religious services for over a century. It's a peaceful place to rest and offers beautiful views of the valley.

You can cross the river at Kings Lake Road to visit Usk, a small mill town on the west bank. If you arrive during the local fair in early August, you can share in a buffalo barbecue. Back on Le Clerc Road, continue past Indian Island and Pioneer Park. Eventually you'll cross the river to Oldtown, Idaho, then go on to Newport.

The Basics

Start: Ione, on Hwy. 31, 4 miles north of Hwy. 20.

Length: 31 miles for Sullivan Lake loop. 52 miles for one-way ride from Ione to Newport. Bicyclists can return to Ione on the same route, or use this ride as part of a longer loop tour.

Terrain: 800-foot climb to Sullivan Lake, otherwise mild grades and good roads.

Food: Stores and restaurants in Ione (start and end point) and Metaline Falls, at 20.7 miles on Sullivan Lake loop. On ride along Pend Oreille River, there is a store and restaurant in Usk at 33.7 miles, requiring a 1-mile detour.

For more information: Ione Chamber of Commerce, P.O. Box 518, Ione, WA 99139; (509) 442–3424. Newport/Oldtown Chamber of Commerce, P.O. Box 1795, Newport, WA 99156; (509) 447–5812.

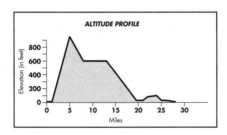

Miles & Directions

First Option, Sullivan Lake loop —

- 0.0 Ride south from Ione on Hwy. 31.
- 0.8 Turn left at Elizabeth Ave. following the Sullivan Lake sign. Cross the river, then bear left on Sullivan Lake Rd.
- 6.0 Summit. From here you descend to Sullivan Lake and follow the lake's west shore.
- 9.2 Noisy Creek Campground; fresh water is available. Follow the Sullivan Lake shoreline.
- 13.5 Take care crossing wood-planked bridge. Pass the West Sullivan campground and ranger station. Continue on road as it descends back toward Pend Oreille River.
- 18.7 Turn left on to Hwy. 31 to Metaline.
- 20.7 Town of Metaline Falls. The old business district is a few blocks to your left. Cross the Pend Oreille River.
- 22.3 Town of Metaline.

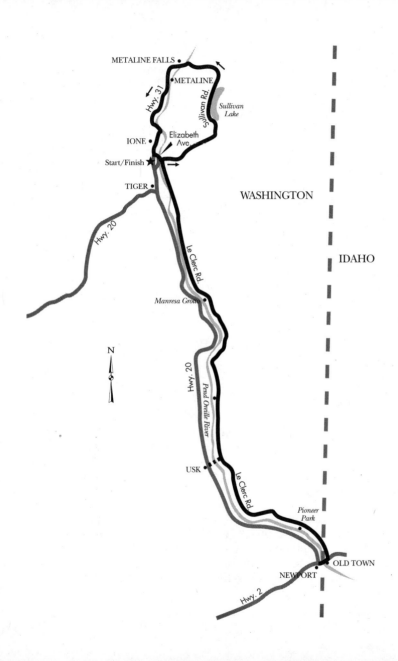

- 27.6 Pass Box Creek Dam rest area.
- 31.1 Return to Ione. Reset odometer for ride to Newport.

Second Option, Newport—

- 0.0 Ride south from Ione on Hwy. 31.
- 0.8 Turn left on Elizabeth Ave. Cross river, turn right onto Le Clerc Road.
- 19.0 Panhandle Campground park; fresh water available.
- 28.0 Manresa Grotto.
- 33.7 To visit Usk, cross the river here. Otherwise continue straight on Le Clerc Rd.
- 48.5 Pass Pioneer Park.
- 51.0 Turn right at stop sign onto Hwy. 2 and cross the Pend Oreille River to Oldtown.
- 52.0 Follow the road left into downtown Newport.

Western Washington

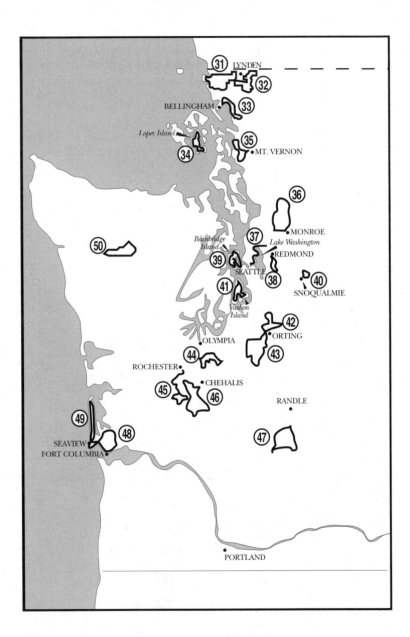

Western Washington

31

West Whatcom County Cruise

Wiser Lake—Lynden—Blaine—Birch Bay—Ferndale

Washington's Nooksack River Valley, just south of the Canadian border, is a fertile region of family-run farms, bordered on the east by foothills and on the west by the inland waters of the Strait of Georgia. The Circum Whatcom County Century, sponsored by Lynden's Spoke Folk bicycling club, consists of two delightful 50-mile loops that highlight very different features of the valley. This late summer event attracts about two hundred bicyclists, who ride either the West Loop, which follows the Puget Sound shoreline, or the East Loop, which explores the Cascade foothills. A few hearty souls ride both, to make a challenging but very rewarding full century.

You'll enjoy riding the quiet country roads, surrounded by fields of berries, grain, and seed potatoes and cows in pastures contentedly chewing their cud. There's much to see: farms, forests, and towns, with a backdrop of mountains to the east and Puget Sound to the west. Farmers in this area are obviously proud of their land. These farms are so charming you'd think they were created simply for the enjoyment of passing bicyclists. You may become a connoisseur of barns: traditional wood barns sheltering cows and swallows, old dilapidated structures slowly sinking back into the earth, and new metal ones filled with farm machinery of all shapes and sizes.

Both loops start at Wiser Lake boat launch. The West Loop

soon passes through the town of Lynden, a quiet community known for its Dutch heritage. Lynden was founded in 1891 by a group of immigrant farmers from the Netherlands led by Phoebe Judson, who became known as "the Mother of Lynden." The rich river-bottom land, similar to what they had known in the old country, allowed the immigrants to prosper. Descendants of these settlers still farm much of the land. The Lynden Pioneer Museum, at Front Street and 3rd, has excellent displays of old farm machinery, toys, and household goods. The museum includes a delightful re-creation of a nineteenth-century Main Street and an impressive collection of antique bicycles (an 1888 Columbia, a 1920s Stutz, and classic Schwinns) to delight any bicycle enthusiast.

From Lynden you'll ride northward to the Canadian border. The international boundary here is nothing more than a ditch, separating a Canadian road to the north from the U.S. road a few feet to the south. Small obelisks are placed every few hundred yards to mark the 48th Parallel. You'll pass the Highway 539 border station and continue west on H Street Road to Blaine. Halfway along this stretch the flat open farmland changes to rolling hills covered with a fir and maple forest. Here you will encounter the only major climb of this ride, fortunately well shaded from the sun. After climbing for 3 miles you'll enjoy a fast 2-mile descent into the town.

Blaine is the I–5 border crossing, making it the busiest station along the western border. Most travelers see little of the town itself as they pass through to their ultimate destination, but Blaine has much to offer. The Peace Arch Park at the border is beautiful, with cheery flower beds and bright green lawns that receive constant, loving care. It's an ideal spot for a rest. Peace Portal Drive, Blaine's main street, has numerous stores, restaurants, and a bakery for hungry bicyclists.

The route follows the shorelines of Drayton Harbor (at the opposite end of the harbor, you can see the Semi-ah-moo Resort at the end of the spit) and Birch Bay southward. These are popular recreation areas. The large bays are full of sailboats, and the beaches are crowded during the summer with children playing in the sand, while gift shops busily sell T-shirts and ice cream. You'll then circle east, past the ARCO petroleum refinery and its tank farms, to the town of Ferndale. After crossing the Nooksack River and I–5, you'll continue along more miles of beautiful flat farmland northward back to Wiser Lake.

The Basics

Start: Wiser Lake Boat Launch 4 miles south of Lynden at the corner of Meridian Guide and Wiser Lake Rd. From Bellingham take Hwy. 539 (Meridian Rd.) north 9 miles to Wiser Lake. The boat launch area has outhouses but no fresh water.

Length: 49.5 miles.

Terrain: Mostly flat riding. There is a moderate 3-mile climb a few miles before Blaine and some low rolling hills past Birch Bay. Most roads used on this route have little traffic, except between Blaine and Birch Bay.

Food: Stores, restaurants, and a bakery in Lynden at 5 miles; a small market at Meridian, at 10.7 miles; full services in Blaine, at 23 miles; several shops along Birch Bay beach, at 30 miles; and full services in the town of Ferndale, at 42 miles.

For more information: Lynden Chamber of Commerce, 1775 Front St., Lynden, WA 98264; (360) 354–5995.

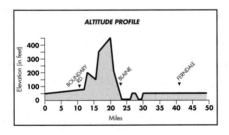

Miles & Directions

- 0.0 Turn right from the Wiser Lake boat-launch parking lot onto W. Wiser Lake Rd., and follow as it meanders east.

- 2.2 Turn left at the stop sign onto Hannegan Rd.
- 4.6 Turn left at the stoplight onto Front St. This is Lynden's main business street.
- 5.6 Turn right at the stoplight onto 17th St. Pass stores to left.
- 5.9 Turn left onto Village Dr.
- 6.1 Turn right onto Double Ditch Rd. This nice flat road with agricultural ditches on each side takes you straight north to the Canadian border.
- 10.1 Double Ditch Rd. dead-ends into Boundary Rd. Turn left, following the border westward.
- 10.7 Turn left onto Guide Meridian Rd. (SR 539), just past the border station and stores.
- 11.2 Turn right onto H St.
- 23.0 Enter Blaine. Turn left on Peace Portal Dr., the town's main commercial street.

To visit Peace Arch Park, turn right on Peace Portal Dr., cross under I–5, then turn left on 2nd St. This beautiful park, famous for multi-colored floral displays, is an excellent rest or picnic stop. This trip adds 1 mile to your mileage.

- 23.5 Turn right onto Bell Rd. (follow signs to Birch Bay), which soon becomes Blaine Rd. Cross the bridge over Dakota Creek.
- 25.5 Turn right onto Drayton Harbor Rd., along the shore land.
- 26.3 Bear left at Y onto Harbor View Rd.
- 27.8 At the bottom of a short descent, turn left onto Birch Bay Dr., the beachfront road.
- 29.0 Turn right then left to stay on Birch Bay Dr.
- 29.3 Bear left onto Jackson Rd. at Y. This takes you south, away from the bay.
- 30.0 Pass Birch Bay State Park.
- 30.8 Cross Grandview Rd. intersection. The ARCO refinery is to your left.
- 31.7 Turn left onto Aldergrove Rd., keeping the refinery to your left.
- 32.5 Just past the refinery, turn right onto Gulf Rd. You are now surrounded by fields and forests.
- 34.5 Turn left onto Henry Rd.

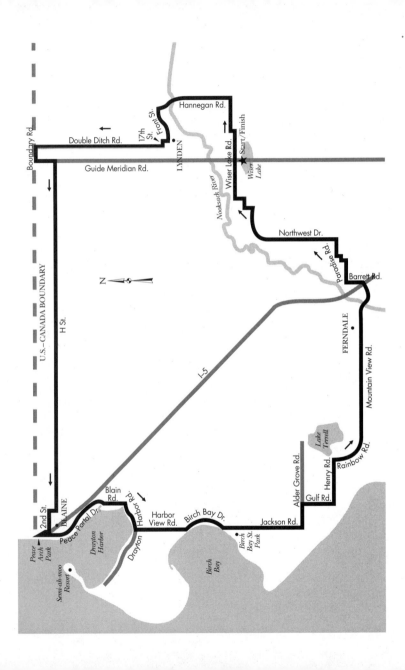

- 34.8 Just after crossing Kickerville Rd., follow Henry as it curves right and becomes Rainbow Rd. You will pass Lake Terrell and wildlife refuge to the left.
- 35.9 Turn left onto Mountain View Rd. Mount Baker is visible ahead if it's a clear day. This road becomes Ferndale's main street.
- 41.5 After riding through Ferndale and over I–5, turn left onto Barrett Rd.
- 42.0 Follow road right on Paradise Rd. and continue through zigzags.
- 43.7 Turn left at stop sign onto Northwest Dr.
- 46.5 Follow road right onto Wiser Lake Rd., which zigzags, then crosses SR 539/Guide Meridian at a stop-sign intersection.
- 49.5 End at Wiser Lake.

32

East Whatcom County Cruise

Wiser Lake—Lawrence—Sumas
Nooksack—Everson—Wiser Lake

The East Loop of the Circum Whatcom County Century explores many miles of farms and forest and meanders along the base of the Cascade foothills. It includes more hills than the West Loop, but the effort is well rewarded with spectacular views. There is usually little traffic on these roads, and the first 10 miles south of Wiser Lake is flat farmland. When you turn onto Noon Road, you'll encounter mild rolling hills as you head in the direction of Mount Baker, one of the major volcanic peaks along the Pacific Coast. On clear days you'll see the mountain's glacier-covered peak just beyond the forested foothills, looming ever closer as you ride east. Baker is a towering white beacon that leads you to the community of Nugent's Corner.

There you'll find a store, café, and most important, the Mount Bakery, a favorite stop for bicyclists, skiers, and climbers heading toward the mountains. Fuel up, you've got plenty of riding ahead. You'll travel north, skirting the foothills. Siper and Goodwin roads are flat, but South and North Pass roads involve some climbing, with impressive views of the valley below and exciting descents. None of the climbs is especially difficult, but together they offer a good workout. Fortunately, the roads have little traffic, and there are plenty of places to stop to rest.

There's a final descent on North Pass Road to the valley flat, then some easy riding through more farmland up to the Canadian border. From this northeast corner you'll head west, through the border town of Sumas. Past Sumas the route goes southward, climbing a small plateau just high enough for a view of the valley below. Soon you are back on the flat valley floor, riding through the village of Nooksack, and along the town's namesake river on Nolte Road for the final stretch to Wiser Lake. What a wonderful ride!

The Basics

Start: Wiser Lake Boat Launch 4 miles south of Lynden at the corner of Meridian Guide and Wiser Lake Rd. From Bellingham take Hwy. 539 (Meridian Rd.) north 9 miles to Wiser Lake. The boat-launch area has outhouses but no fresh water.
Length: 50.2 miles.
Terrain: Flat to moderate hills.
Food: Store, café, and bakery, at 17 miles; store and restaurants in Sumas, at 32 miles; store in Nooksack, at 42 miles.
For more information: Spoke Folk, P.O. Box 688, Lynden, WA 98264.

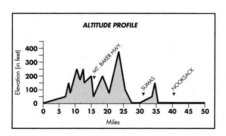

Miles & Directions

- 0.0 Turn left from the Wiser Lake boat-launch parking lot onto Wiser Lake Rd. Cross Guide Meridian at stop-sign intersection.

- 0.6 Turn left onto Old Guide Rd. Follow this south, crossing West Pole and King Tut Rd.
- 3.7 Turn left onto Hemmi Rd.
- 8.2 Turn right onto Noon Rd., into rolling hills.
- 10.4 Turn left onto E. Smith Rd.
- 14.8 Turn left on the Mount Baker Hwy. (SR 542).
- 15.8 After crossing the Nooksack River, turn left on Hwy. 9. Grocery, café, and Mount Bakery at corner.
- 17.0 Turn right onto Siper Rd. Cross railroad tracks carefully.
- 18.8 Follow road right onto Hopewell, and then left onto Goodwin Rd.
- 21.6 Turn right at stop sign onto S. Pass Rd.
- 23.4 Turn left onto N. Pass Rd.
- 25.3 Turn right at stop sign to stay on N. Pass Rd. as it jogs east, then north.
- 26.8 Turn right onto Telegraph Rd. at stop sign.
- 28.1 Bear right on N. Telegraph Rd. (straight becomes Hovel Rd.).
- 28.4 Bear left at stop sign onto Sumas Rd.
- 28.8 Turn right at stop sign onto Rock Rd.
- 29.5 Turn left onto Conchman Rd.
- 30.0 Turn left at stop sign onto Jones Rd., which becomes Garfield St. through the town of Sumas.
- 31.2 Cross Cherry St. (SR 9), with the border crossing and grocery store to your right. Ride carefully over five sets of railroad tracks, then bear right at Y and take an immediate left onto Kneumann Rd.
- 32.4 Road turns left and becomes Barbo Rd.
- 32.9 Turn right at stop sign onto SR 546; in 100 yards continue straight onto Halverstick Rd., where the highway curves left.
- 34.4 Turn left onto Swanson Rd.
- 35.5 Turn right at stop sign onto Clearbrook Rd.
- 35.9 Turn left at stop sign onto Van Buren Rd. Take care riding over angled railroad tracks 0.5 mile farther.
- 37.8 Turn left at T onto Lindsay Rd. In 0.5 mile cross Nooksack Rd. (SR 9), and continue on Lindsay Rd.
- 39.0 Turn right at stop sign onto Gillies Rd. Follow this as it

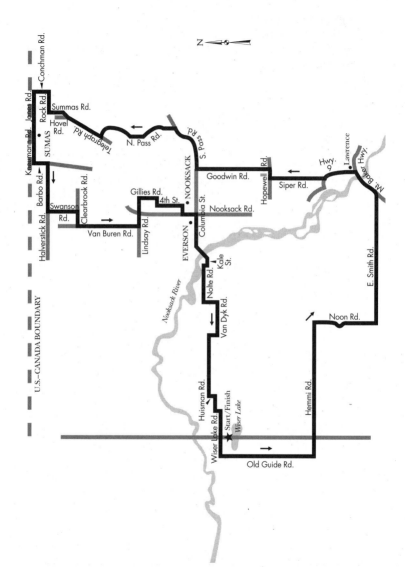

zigzags and becomes Nooksack's 4th St.

- 40.5 Turn right onto Breckenridge Rd./Madison St. through the town of Nooksack. Turn left at stop sign next to city park onto Nooksack Rd. (SR 9).
- 41.4 Turn right onto SR 544, which becomes Main St. through Everson.
- 42.2 Continue on SR 544 as it curves left and crosses the Nooksack River to become Everson Rd.
- 42.9 Bear right onto Kale St., to continue on SR 544.
- 43.1 Where 544 curves left, turn right onto Mead Ave. Follow road left onto Nolte Rd. Stay on Nolte as it curves left again.
- 45.0 Turn right at stop sign onto Van Dyk Rd. Follow Van Dyk as it jogs right and then left, across Hannegan Rd. at a stop-sign intersection.
- 48.3 Follow road left onto Huisman Rd.
- 48.6 Turn right onto Wiser Lake Rd.
- 49.0 Follow Wiser as it curves left, then right.
- 50.2 End back at Wiser Lake boat launch.

33

Chuckanut Drive Cruise

Fairhaven—Chuckanut Drive—Alger
Lake Samish—Fairhaven

Chuckanut Drive is a gorgeous road that winds between the Chuckanut Mountain Range and the shores of Samish Bay, south from the City of Bellingham to the Skagit Valley. Along the way riders enjoy spectacular views of the islands and inland waters off the northwest Washington coast. At one time Chuckanut Drive was the main road south of Bellingham. It is now a scenic highway, popular with tourists, car-commercial photographers, and, of course, bicyclists. On weekend mornings riders often congregate at Tony's Café or the Marketplace Building in Bellingham's Fairhaven commercial district, in preparation for a ride down Chuckanut. The experienced local cyclists like to get an early start, since tourist traffic, heavy on sunny afternoons, distracts from what is otherwise an ideal bicycle ride.

Fairhaven was one of the four original towns that eventually formed the City of Bellingham. It still retains much of its turn-of-the-century charm. If this is your first visit, allow some time to explore its old brick buildings, small shops, and friendly restaurants. The fine Terminal Building at 11th and Harris was built in 1888 of bricks that were originally carried as ballast from Asia. The Marketplace Building, built in 1890, once housed a men's club that hosted visiting celebrities, including Mark Twain. It has recently been rebuilt into a charming shopping and eating mall.

Chuckanut Drive begins at the beautiful flower gardens of

Fairhaven Park, one of several Pacific Northwest parks designed by the famous Olmsted brothers. The road follows the shoreline of Chuckanut Bay out of town. It's a curvy and hilly ride, offering excitement, beauty, and plenty of challenges. Bicyclists with fat tires and a preference for slow and quiet riding can choose the 5-mile-long Interurban Trail, which parallels Chuckanut Drive through brilliant green forests and glens to Larrabee State Park, Washington's oldest state park. The park's saltwater public beaches, wooded trails, and green lawns offer numerous opportunities for picnics, resting, and fun.

South of Larrabee Park, Chuckanut Drive winds along the cliffs between Samish Bay and the evergreen forests of Chuckanut Mountain. There are several viewpoints along the way, offering magnificent vistas of the islands and waterways offshore. If you've already worked up an appetite, you can stop at the Oyster Creek Inn or Chuckanut Manor Restaurant for a hearty lunch.

After about 10 miles Chuckanut Drive descends onto the Samish Flats. The most popular return routes involve climbing Colony Road or Bow Hill to Old Highway 99, past the small community of Alger, then north to Samish Lake. The west side of Samish Lake, farther away from the freeway, is the preferred side to ride. It also provides access to Samish County Park, where you can stop for a rest or swim. Leaving the lake there is one more climb to Old Samish Way, then a descent past Padden Lake Park. Where Samish Way curves right, the route turns onto Wilkin Street, and takes a wonderful zigzag route down the hillside back to Fairhaven.

The Basics

Start: 12th St. and Harris Ave. in the Fairhaven Shopping District of Bellingham. Take I–5 exit 250, then drive west on Old Fairhaven Parkway 1 mile to 12th St.
Length: 32.2 or 43 miles.
Terrain: Hilly and windy roads, especially along Chuckanut Dr.
Food: Oyster Creek Inn at 9.3 miles; Chuckanut Manor Restaurant

at 10.6 miles; Alger Tavern and Food Mart at 18.4 miles; and Al & Carmins Market at 26.4 miles. On the 43-mile ride, Chuckanut Valley Store and the excellent Rhododendron Café are in Bow at 13.3 miles.

For more information: Bellingham Visitors Bureau, 904 Potter St., Bellingham, WA 98226; (360) 671–3990.

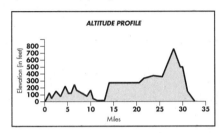

Miles & Directions

- 0.0 Ride south on 12th St. In 0.2 mile cross a small bridge over Padden Creek, then bear left at the Fairhaven Park Rose Garden onto Chuckanut Dr.
- 1.7 To reach the Interurban Trail, turn left onto Lake Samish Rd. to Arroyo Park. The trail passes through the park and continues for 5 miles south to Larrabee State Park.
- 5.0 Larrabee State Park entrance.
- 11.7 Turn left onto Colony Rd. Follow Colony as it curves right, then left, up into the wooded hills.

For a 43-mile ride, continue 1.6 miles farther on Chuckanut Dr. to Bow. Turn left onto Bow Hill Rd. Cross under I–5, then turn left (north) on Old Hwy. 99. In about 1.0 mile bear left onto Friday Creek Rd., a beautiful old road that meanders through the woods to Alger. Follow instructions from 18.8 miles.

- 18.4 Turn right at T onto Lake Samish Rd.
- 18.8 Alger. Turn left (north) on Old Hwy. 99.
- 21.4 Cross under I–5, continue straight on Nulle Rd.

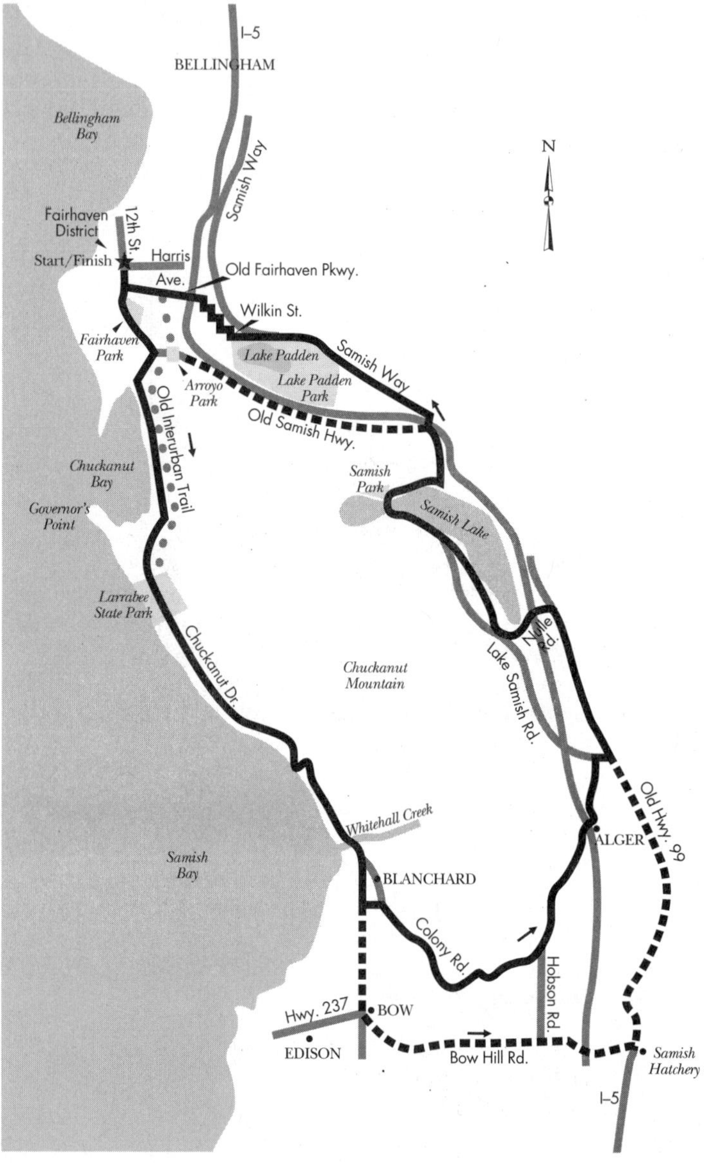

I-5
BELLINGHAM
Bellingham Bay
Samish Way
N
Fairhaven District
12th St.
Start/Finish
Harris Ave.
Old Fairhaven Pkwy.
Wilkin St.
Fairhaven Park
Lake Padden
Lake Padden Park
Samish Way
Arroyo Park
Old Interurban Trail
Old Samish Hwy.
Chuckanut Bay
Governor's Point
Samish Park
Samish Lake
Larrabee State Park
Chuckanut Dr.
Chuckanut Mountain
Nulle Rd.
Lake Samish Rd.
Old Hwy. 99
Whitehall Creek
ALGER
Samish Bay
BLANCHARD
Colony Rd.
Hobson Rd.
Hwy. 237
BOW
EDISON
Bow Hill Rd.
Samish Hatchery
I-5

- 22.0 Turn right on W. Lake Samish.
- 24.6 Follow road as it curves right and across bridge. Samish Park is on opposite shore.
- 25.5 Bear left onto Old Samish Hwy.

An easier alternative route (it avoids traffic and a big climb) is to turn left just before I–5 on Old Samish Hwy., an enjoyable curvy road that descends to Arroyo Park and back to Chuckanut Dr. Turn right at Chuckanut for the 1.7-mile ride back to Fairhaven.

- 26.5 Cross I–5, continue on Samish Way, up a hill, then down past Lake Padden Park.
- 29.6 Where Samish Way curves right, away from Lake Padden Park, bear left onto Wilkin St. Follow this road as it zigzags down the hill, becoming 40th, Broad, 38th, Harrison, 37th, South, 36th, and Connelly Ave.
- 30.9 Cross under I–5. The road becomes Old Fairhaven Pkwy.
- 32.2 Turn right on 12th St. End in 2 blocks back at Harris.

34

Lopez Island Ramble

Ferry Dock—Lopez Village—Shark Reef
Agate Beach—Spencer Spit—Ferry Dock

Lopez is considered the best of the San Juan Islands for bicycling, especially for beginners. It is the flattest of the islands and retains a rural character, with numerous working farms, secluded homes, and a number of waterfront parks. Lopez is the first ferry stop from Anacortez, making it a natural starting point for island adventures.

The favorite route is to circle the island counterclockwise, which puts riders on the shore side of the roadway for the best views. This is desirable, because every curve of the shoreline offers another exciting and gorgeous ocean vista. This route also gives riders a chance to purchase supplies in the town of Lopez toward the beginning of the ride.

As with most islands there is a steep climb leaving the ferry landing. Odlin County Park is conveniently located a mile from the terminal. This pleasant waterfront park includes a beach, play areas, and several secluded hiker/biker campsites. It is a popular overnight stop for bicyclists. For reservations call (206) 468–2496.

Your next stop is the village of Lopez. Here you will find a supermarket, a choice of restaurants, the Holly "B" Bakery, and other small shops. Don't miss the Lopez Historical Museum, where you can learn about the island's history, local fishing techniques, and other unique features of the island. The museum is open Friday to Sunday, 12:00 4:00 P.M. Call (206) 468–2049 for more information.

Follow the shore of Fisherman Bay, past a resort and the Lopez Bicycle Works bike shop. A 0.5-mile detour along the bay's south shore leads to Otis Perkins Park, with a public pebble beach overlooking the San Juan Channel. This is a good lookout for killer whales. Continuing south, you ride through a rolling countryside of pastures and forests to the southwest corner of the island. Shark Reef Wildlife Sanctuary is one of the island's highlights. Wander down to the shore for beautiful views and a unique coastline. This is an excellent location for watching bald eagles, shorebirds, and fascinating intertidal life.

Continue south, along Mackaye Harbor, where the fishing fleets dock and fishing families camp, to Agate Beach, a perfect lunch site. Just off the beach is Iceberg Island. In clear weather you can see the Olympic Mountains to the south and Vancouver Island due west.

You'll next loop north past Mud Bay and Islandale and take Center Road north through the middle of the island to the Lopez Elementary School. The route turns toward the shore on School Road, then zigzags up to Spencer Spit State Park.

The park includes several camping sites set aside for hikers and bicyclists. It's also a pleasant place to picnic and explore, with informative displays on the human and natural history of the area. The beaches along the sand spit are a good place to stretch legs tired from bicycling.

From Spencer Spit it's another 2.5 miles of great riding back to the ferry terminal.

The Basics

Start: Lopez Island Ferry Terminal, at the north tip of the island. You can visit for just a day or stay on the island. San Juan ferries leave several times each day from Anacortes, Washington, and four times each day from Sidney, British Columbia.
Length: 33.5 miles.

Terrain: As with all of the San Juan Islands, rolling hills are covered with fields and forests. This is considered the flattest of the major islands, but wide-range gearing is still recommended due to numerous short but steep climbs.

Food: Stores, restaurants, and a bakery in Lopez Village, at 4.3 miles; Islandale Store at 19 miles.

For more information: Lopez Island Chamber of Commerce, P.O. Box 121, Lopez, WA 98261; (360) 468–3800.

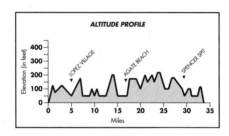

Miles & Directions

- 0.0 Take Ferry Rd. south from the terminal. Bicyclists are usually asked to wait at the side of the roadway until motor-vehicle traffic passes; after that, the road generally has little traffic. There is a short, steep climb and then a quick descent during the first mile.
- 1.2 Odlin Park turnoff at right.
- 2.1 Where Ferry Rd. dead-ends, turn right onto Fisherman Bay Rd.
- 2.6 Continue straight (where Fisherman Bay Rd. curves left) onto Lopez Rd. Either road will take you to the village of Lopez, but Lopez Rd. has better views and less traffic.
- 4.2 Village of Lopez. After stopping continue east on Lopez Rd.
- 4.5 Turn right onto Fisherman Bay Rd. Follow the shore of Fisherman Bay.

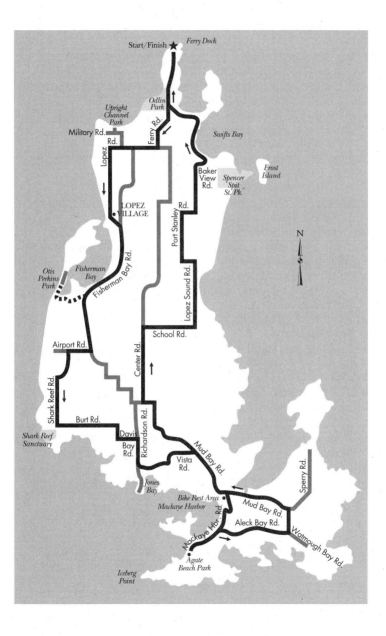

- 6.0 Otis Perkins Park (turn right onto Bayshore Rd.) is a .5-mile detour. Otherwise continue straight.
- 7.1 Right onto Airport Rd. You will pass the golf course and Lopez Airport on your right.
- 7.5 Turn left onto Shark Reef Rd. At the end of this road is the trail to Shark Reef Wildlife Sanctuary.
- 9.3 Left onto Burt Rd.
- 10.0 Go straight onto Davis Bay Rd., and continue on it through two jogs.
- 11.0 Right onto Richardson Rd.
- 12.0 Turn around where Richardson Rd. ends at Jones Bay.
- 12.5 Right onto Vista Rd.
- 13.7 Right onto Mud Bay Rd.
- 14.6 Right onto Mackaye Harbor Rd. There is a Bike Rest Area behind the fire station.
- 16.4 Agate Beach County Park. Turn around.
- 17.3 Right turn onto Aleck Bay Rd. Follow the road when it curves left.
- 19.4 Left onto Mud Bay Rd.
- 23.0 Follow road left, then turn right onto Center Rd.
- 24.7 Just past the Lopez Public School, turn right onto School Rd.
- 25.7 Left onto Lopez Sound Rd. Follow it as it turns left.
- 27.0 Right onto Port Stanley Rd.
- 28.7 Right onto Baker View Rd. for a visit to Spencer Spit Park.
- 29.5 Turn around at Spencer Spit State Park.
- 30.0 Right onto Port Stanley Rd., which curves left past Swifts Bay.
- 32.3 Right onto Ferry Rd.
- 33.5 Return to Lopez Ferry Dock.

35

Mount Vernon Cruise

Mt. Vernon—Fir Island—Padilla Bay
Edison—Bow—Mt. Vernon

The Northwest Bicycle Touring Society's Mount Vernon Century, established in 1968, is one of the oldest annual bicycle rides in the Pacific Northwest. It is held each September as part of the League of American Bicyclists' National Century Month. It's a beautiful ride across the brilliant green Skagit River delta, along the windy shore of Padilla Bay, and through the historic Samish Valley. Using low-traffic farm roads over the flat valleys, the Mount Vernon Century route, which requires two loops of this route, has delighted bicyclists for more than two decades.

The ride begins in Mt. Vernon and follows Dike Road along the Britt Slough and the South Fork of the Skagit River to the small community of Conway. You can climb up onto the dike to enjoy views of the river and farmlands below. From Conway the route crosses onto Fir Island, part of the river delta. Fir Island includes the Skagit Wildlife Area, an extensive refuge that serves as an important resting point for birds on their annual migrations. Watch for deer, muskrat, foxes, coyotes, hawks, and all kinds of migrating birds as you ride through the quiet farmland.

The route crosses the Skagit River's north fork back to the mainland, continuing north through valley farmlands, then follows the shoreline of Padilla Bay. You can choose either the 2-mile-long, gravel Padilla Bay Path, or continue on the roadway. Along this stretch you'll enjoy watching boats sailing in the bay; beyond are the San Juan Islands and the Anacortes oil-refining structures. A few miles farther you'll pass Bayview State Park, used as a checkpoint and refreshment stop during the Century ride. The sandy beach makes a pleasant rest and picnic spot. You can also visit the Breazeale Padilla Bay Wildlife Interpretive Center, one-half mile past the park, to learn more about the natural history of this fascinating region.

The route zigzags through Edison, a small farming and artists' community. Bicyclists looking for a meal can choose among the Edison Inn, Longhorn Saloon, or the Edison Café, which offers homemade pies and soups. A little farther you'll pass through the village of Bow and the serene Bow Cemetery, where the route turns south through farmlands, past the little town of Avon, toward Mt. Vernon. You'll enter Mt. Vernon on McLean Road, a designated bike route with an excellent shoulder. To avoid some of the city traffic, the route takes a zigzag course through residential streets, then crosses the Skagit River into downtown. You may want to take advantage of this opportunity to explore Mt. Vernon's historic and vibrant city center before continuing back to your starting point at the fairgrounds.

The Basics

Start: Mt. Vernon Fairgrounds, at Cleveland and Hazel St. From I–5, take exit 226 in downtown Mt. Vernon. Go west on Kincaid .2 mile, and turn left on Cleveland. Go .5 mile south until the intersection with Hazel St.

Length: 48.5 or 23.2 miles.

Terrain: Roads range from good to excellent, very flat.

Food: Farmhouse Restaurant at 22.6 miles; Edison Inn Restaurant, Longhorn Saloon, and Edison Café in Edison, at 33 miles; Rhododendron Café at 34 miles; and stores at 14.1, 34, and 38.7 miles.

For more information: Northwest Bicycle Touring Society, 6166 92nd Ave. SE, Mercer Island, WA 98040.

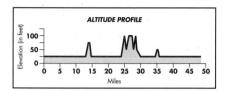

Miles & Directions

- 0.0 West on Hazel.
- 0.4 Just after road curves left at the water-treatment plant, turn right on Dike Rd.
- 6.2 Turn right on Fir Island Rd. Cross Skagit River, and take the first right onto Skagit City Rd.
- 10.4 Road curves left, becomes Dry Slough Rd.
- 11.5 Turn right onto Moore Rd.
- 12.8 Stay right to follow dike.
- 13.6 Turn right onto Chilberg Rd. and take bridge over the Skagit River.
- 14.1 Turn right onto Summer Dr.
- 14.6 Left onto Bradshaw Rd.
- 18.4 Cross McLean Rd.

For the 23-mile ride, turn right on McLean Rd., go 2 miles to Avon-Allen Rd., and follow instructions starting at 45.7 miles.

- 20.0 At stop-sign intersection with Hwy. 20, turn left onto Young Rd. as the highway curves right. Most bicyclists simply ride on the left shoulder.
- 22.2 Right at stop sign onto Whitney Rd.
- 22.7 Cross Hwy. 20, cross railroad tracks, and follow road as it curves right.
- 23.0 Road curves left, becomes Bayview-Edison Rd.
- 23.5 Padilla Bay Path. You can take this mostly gravel path for 2 miles or continue on roadway.
- 25.3 Padilla Bay Path rejoins Bayview-Edison Rd.
- 26.3 Bayview State Park.

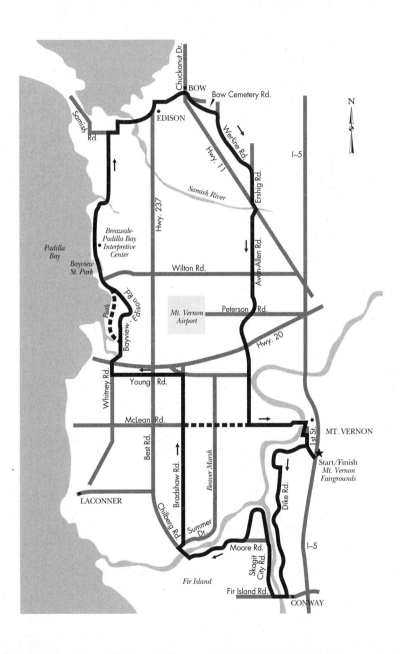

- 26.8 Breazeale Padilla Bay Interpretive Center.
- 30.9 Turn right at intersection with Samish Rd. to continue on Bayview-Edison Rd. The road zigzags and crosses the Samish River.
- 32.6 Turn left at stop sign onto Hwy. 237, and follow the highway as it zigzags through the small community of Edison. Turn left in front of the Edison Inn, right at Longhorn Saloon, and bear left at the Edison Café.
- 34.0 Cross Hwy. 11/Chuckanut Dr. at Bow.
- 35.0 Turn right on Bow Cemetery Rd.
- 35.4 Turn right at cemetery onto Werline Rd.
- 37.4 Turn right, onto Ershig Rd.
- 38.5 Turn left at stop sign onto Hwy. 11. Cross the Samish River on a low bridge, then turn right onto Avon-Allen Rd.
- 41.9 Cross Peterson Rd.
- 43.0 Cross Hwy. 20.
- 45.7 Left at stop sign on McLean Rd.
- 47.2 Turn right on S. Wall St., left on Garfield St., left on S. Baker St.
- 47.5 Turn right onto Division St. Cross the Skagit River into Mt. Vernon.
- 47.7 Turn right on Main St., first turn after bridge.
- 48.0 Left on Kincaid St. (at Moose Lodge), then a quick right onto 1st St.
- 48.5 End back at fairgrounds.

36

McClinchy Mile Challenge

Monroe—Snohomish—Granite Falls
Lake Roesiger—Monroe

The McClinchy Mile is a popular bike ride held the Saturday closest to St Patrick's Day. It is sponsored by the Everett, Washington, bike club: BIKES (Biker's Ideal Kinematic Exploration Society). How far is a McClinchy Mile? According to the registration form:

> *An in-depth search of Scottish folklore by BIKES Tour Committee could not yield an exact distance contained in a McClinchy Mile. However, we have narrowed it down to somewhere between 21 and 175 miles. We leave its exact distance for you to determine . . . BEGORRAH!*

Participants can choose from six loops, including a 32-mile off-road option. When the weather is good, the McClinchy Mile attracts about a thousand riders to the Monroe Fairgrounds, 30 miles northeast of Seattle, to enjoy very fine bicycling through beautiful, farm-filled valleys and gentle, rolling, forest-covered hills just west of the Cascade Mountains. The ride described here is the 48-mile route to Granite Falls, with an additional 22-mile option to Arlington.

All routes begin by passing through downtown Monroe, a medium-size town near the junction of the Skykomish and Snohomish rivers. Monroe was established in 1858 as a mill town and commercial center for area farmers. It is now best known for the

Twin River Correction Facility, established in 1907, one of the largest state prisons in Washington State. This route passes the prison; its high fences, sheer walls, and gun towers are a grim contrast to the lighthearted freedom that bicyclists enjoy on this spring-day ride.

Crossing under Highway 522, the road becomes the Old Snohomish-Monroe Highway, which leads to the town of Snohomish. Snohomish is an especially pleasant community with a unique history. It was first settled by E. C. Ferguson, who selected the site where the Snohomish and Pilchuck rivers join, in hopes of establishing a river ferry. Through the years "Old Ferg" served as saloon owner, county commissioner, auditor, justice of the peace, judge, postmaster, and superintendent of schools. The township was surveyed in 1867 and became a center of logging, lumber mills, and vegetable canneries. When a railroad line arrived in 1888, the *Snohomish Eye* newspaper celebrated with this verse:

> *New sidewalks and bridges our village will have,*
> *And all business will go with a hum,*
> *Quick change from a village to city we'll have*
> *When the Lake Shore and Eastern is done.*

The old downtown (1st Avenue), with scores of antique shops, and historical neighborhoods of Victorian-era homes (avenues A to E) indicate that the railroad brought prosperity. The Blackman House (118 Avenue B, built in 1878), once home of innovative logger Hyrcanus Blackman, is now a public museum.

Continuing north, riders pass through the small community of Machias. Just past the Granville Grange, bicyclists going all of the way to Arlington turn left on Burn Road, others turn right for the shorter route directly to Granite Falls. The quiet main street of this small town, normally populated with pickup trucks, is suddenly crowded with colorful lightweight bicycles. Amused store clerks and waitresses serve the dozens of hungry Lycra-clothed bicyclists. After eating you may want to stop at the community's small Historical Museum, at Wabash and Union.

The ride back to Monroe over wooded hills skirts Lake Roesiger. Cyclists can choose either the flatter west side or the east side, which passes Lake Roesiger Park. The rest of the route is relatively flat and easy. Soon you are again riding on Main Street through downtown Monroe and back to the fairgrounds. There hundreds of self-satisfied cyclists are congratulating one another, swapping stories and descriptions of the various McClinchy Mile options.

The Basics

Start: Monroe Fairgrounds. From the Seattle area take Hwy. 522 through Bothell to Monroe. Where 522 ends, turn right on Hwy. 2, .5 mile to the fairgrounds.
Length: 48 or 70 miles.
Terrain: Moderate hills and traffic on rural roads.
Food: Stores and restaurants in Snohomish, at 8.2 miles; Machias Grocery Store at 14 miles; convenience store at 19.5 miles; stores and restaurants in Granite Falls, at 23.5 miles.
For more information: BIKES, P.O. Box 5242, Everett, WA 98206.

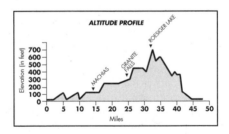

Miles & Directions

- 0.0 Exit fairgrounds, go south on 179th Ave. into Monroe.
- 1.0 Turn right on Main St. (163rd. St.).
- 1.8 Pass Monroe's Twin River Prison, then pass under Hwy.

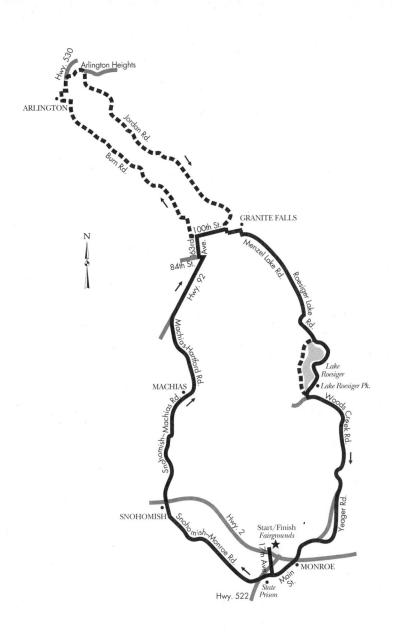

522. Continue straight on Snohomish-Monroe Rd.

- 8.2 Enter the town of Snohomish. Turn right at stop sign on 2nd St., then an immediate left onto Pine St.
- 8.7 Take care crossing angled railroad tracks, then turn right onto Maple. Continue on this road as it changes name to Snohomish-Machias Rd.
- 13.0 Bear right at stop sign onto Machias Cutoff.
- 14.1 Machias. Bear left at OK Mill onto Machias-Hartford Rd.
- 17.5 Turn right at stop sign onto Hwy. 92.
- 20.7 Turn left on 84th St., then take a quick right onto 163rd Ave.
- 21.9 Turn right onto Burn Rd. (100th Ave.).

For 70-mile option, turn left on Burn Rd. (100th Ave.). Follow Burn Rd. as it curves right, left, and right to Arlington, at 31.0 miles. Turn left on 1st Ave., then right onto Macleod St., which becomes Hwy. 530. At 32.9 miles turn right onto Arlington Heights, and turn right on Jordan Rd. at 33.9 miles. At 46.0 miles you enter Granite Falls; follow directions below.

- 23.4 Turn right at stop sign onto Jordan Rd. In 0.3 miles turn left at stop sign on W. Stanley St. (Hwy. 92) through Granite Falls.
- 24.3 Turn right on Alder Ave., then turn left at stop sign onto Menzel Lake Rd. (92nd).
- 31.4 Bear left on Roesiger Lake Rd., or turn right onto W. Lake Roesiger Rd., which is flatter but misses Lake Roesiger Park.
- 33.8 Lake Roesiger Park.
- 35.0 Turn left at stop sign on Woods Creek Rd.
- 44.0 Bear left at Yeager Rd.
- 45.8 Bear left at stop sign on Woods Creek.
- 45.7 Cross Hwy. 2, then turn right onto Old Owen Rd., which becomes Main St. in Monroe.
- 47.0 Turn right on 179th Ave.
- 48.0 Cross Hwy. 2, and return to fairgrounds.

37

Seattle Trail Ramble

Gas Works Park—Lake Washington—Bothell
Woodenville Wineries—Redmond

This ride takes advantage of the excellent trail system that meanders through King County, connecting urban Seattle with the Marymoor Park Velodrome in the city of Redmond. The route offers more than 25 miles of delightful bicycling separated from motor-vehicle traffic. Along the way you'll see Seattle at its best and enjoy the beauty of the quiet countryside. It's a popular ride among the city's cyclists.

The people of Seattle love their trails. You'll share them with joggers, skaters, walkers, equestrians, fishermen, wildlife, and every type of bicyclist imaginable: from children taking their first ride to serious racers on a hard day of training. It's a happy, colorful parade.

This trail system began in 1973 when the city purchased 9 miles of abandoned railroad right-of-way from the Burlington Northern Railway. It has proven to be a great success: On a typical summer day more than two thousand people, mostly bicyclists, use the trail. It is popular with bicycle commuters; University of Washington officials report that the cost of paving the trail has been repaid in the university's reduced parking costs alone. A city study showed that the trail's popularity has increased the value of homes adjacent to it.

The success of this project encouraged the development of more trails, and the system continues to grow. In recent years links have extended west toward the Puget Sound waterfront and eastward toward the Cascade Mountains. Soon bicyclists will be able to ride from Seattle across the Cascades and through eastern Washington entirely on trails.

This route begins at Gas Works Park on the north shore of Lake Union. Old rusting machinery in the park, which once produced residential stove gas, now frames the Seattle skyline. You'll follow the Burke Gilman Trail from the park to the University of Washington, past the University Medical Center, Husky Stadium, and other campus landmarks. The trail continues through suburban Seattle, along the shoreline of Lake Washington. You can stop to rest along the way at several parks.

The Burke Gilman trail ends at Logboom Park. From there you'll pass through an industrial area along the north shore of Lake Washington and continue east on the Sammamish River Trail. Soon you will find yourself riding along the quiet Sammamish River to the city of Bothell. There you can stop at Bothell Landing, a local historical park, accessible to the trail by an arched wood bridge over the river. The landing includes frontier village homes and a variety of displays on local history and traditional crafts.

A few miles out of Bothell, the trail passes within a half mile of two wineries that welcome visitors to tour the facilities, sample wines, and picnic on the landscaped grounds. To the left you will see the palatial Chateau Ste. Michelle winery, to the right is the charming Victorian-style Columbia winery. Bicyclists, even those who don't drink wine, often stop for lunch. The Ste. Michelle winery sponsors public concerts on its lawn during the summer, and a deli supplies light snacks. Both wineries are open year-round from 10:00 A.M. to 5:00 P.M. Call (206) 488–1133 for more information.

On the last stretch of trail before Redmond, you are likely to see people fishing, paddling canoes, or birding along the Sammamish River. The trail continues through the city of Redmond to Marymoor Park, which offers a lot to see and do, from museums to hiking trails, but most bicyclists "hightail it" to the velodrome. One of the few such facilities in the United States, it is the site of many national and international bicycling competitions. The track is open to all users, provided that you wear a helmet and follow safety rules. If you have any energy left, this is your chance to test your speed and bike-handling skills.

Marymoor Park is a popular starting point for additional rides, such as the Lake Sammamish Ramble described next. Return to Seattle the way you came.

The Basics

Start: Gas Works Park, on the north side of Lake Union, in Seattle. Take 45th St. west from I–5, then turn left on Meridian or Wallingford Ave. until they end at the park.

Length: 24 miles (round-trip to Logboom Park), 42 miles (round-trip to Ste. Michelle Winery), or 51 miles (round-trip to Marymoor Park Velodrome).

Terrain: Flat and easy trail, excellent for beginners. Due to heavy pedestrian and bicycle traffic, parts of this route are not suitable for fast riding.

Food: Many options, including restaurants at Bothell Landing, at 15 miles; deli food available at the Chateau Ste. Michelle, at 19 miles; and restaurants in Redmond, at 23.8 miles.

For more information: The Seattle Bicycle Program (206) 684–7584 and the King County Roadshare Program (206) 296–RIDE provide bicycling information and maps.

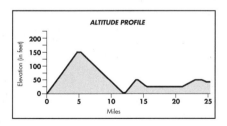

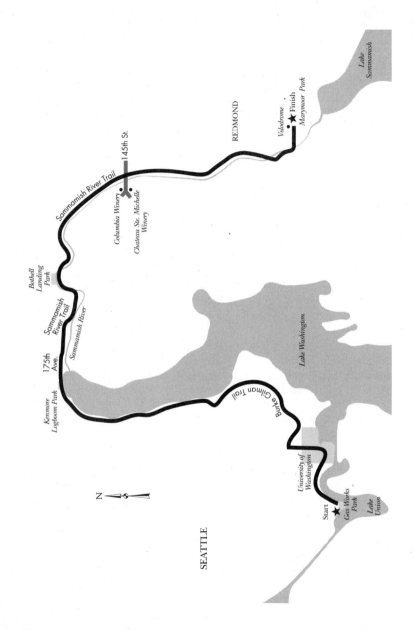

Miles & Directions

- 0.0 Turn right (east) on the Burke Gilman Trail across North-lake Way from Gas Works Park. Cross under the towering I–5 bridge and through the University of Washington campus.
- 2.9 Cross 25th Ave. NE.
- 7.1 Mathews Beach Park.
- 12.0 Logboom Park/Tracy Owen Station. Continue east along NE 175th St.
- 13.5 Join the Sammamish River Trail. Follow the trail along the Sammamish River.
- 15.2 Pass Bothell Landing historical park.
- 19.0 Public rest rooms and a drinking fountain adjacent to the trail. Turn right onto NE 145th St. to visit the Ste. Michelle and Columbia wineries, visible 0.5 mile west, at the base of the hill.
- 24.0 Follow trail as it turns right to cross the Sammamish River, then left across Leary Way.
- 24.8 Here the trail ends at the entrance to Marymoor Park. Turn left into the park, past the Willowmoor Farm Museum (the park office there is a good place to obtain additional information), and continue toward the towering lights of the velodrome.
- 25.5 End at the velodrome.

Lake Sammamish Ramble

Marymoor—Lake Sammamish State Park—Marymoor

A bicycle racetrack is called a "velodrome," and one of the few velodromes in the United States is at Marymoor Park, at the north end of Lake Sammamish in Redmond. The Marymoor Velodrome has been the site of major national and international racing events. It is well used for regular weekly races and endless practice by bicyclists who want to test themselves and develop track-riding skills.

The velodrome is an exciting place to visit. Track racing is bicycling in its purest form. Even nonracers enjoy watching riders circle gracefully around and around the steeply banked velodrome, practicing bike handling and sparring with other riders. The velodrome and its location at the urban fringe make Redmond a popular place for bicycling. The city is working to develop these attributes; Redmond calls itself the "Bicycle Capital of the Northwest," and local activists are working to create a National Bicycle Center alongside the velodrome. It will include a museum and facilities for a variety of bicycling activities.

Almost any summer day you'll see bicyclists assembling at Marymoor for adventures. The Lake Sammamish Ramble is one of the most popular routes, following the Sammamish Parkway around the lake. This route is equally popular with families out for an afternoon of easy riding and racers taking a quick loop. Counterclockwise riding is recommended because much of the shoreside lane of the Sammamish Parkway lacks a shoulder.

Although the lake is surrounded by residential developments, there are still many opportunities to admire its beauty, including several parks along the way. The largest of these is Lake Sammamish State Park, at the southern end, an ideal rest stop. When you've finished riding take time to explore Marymoor Park. In addition to the velodrome, you'll find a restored turn-of-the-century farm, hiking trails, and the beginning of the National Bicycle Center.

The Basics

Start: Marymoor Park Velodrome. Take Hwy. 520 from Seattle or Bellevue to the Sammamish Parkway exit in Redmond. Turn south from the highway, then left in .1 mile into Marymoor Park. Follow signs to the velodrome.

Length: 23 miles.

Terrain: Suburban roads with generally good shoulders or bike lanes. A few hills.

Food: The Little Store grocery at 7.5 miles; store and restaurants at 10.2 miles; convenience store at 14.8 miles.

For more information: King County Roadshare program (206–296–RIDE) provides county bicycling maps and other information.

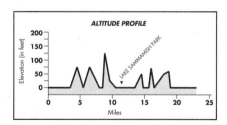

Miles & Directions

- 0.0 Turn right (west) from the velodrome parking lot.
- 0.7 Turn left onto W. Lake Sammamish Pkwy.
- 1.7 Bear left to stay on W. Lake Sammamish Pkwy.

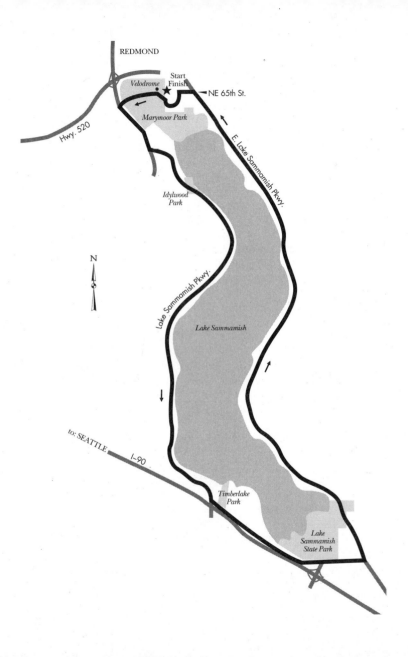

- 7.5 Pass The Little Store grocery.
- 8.7 Turn left to stay on W. Lake Sammamish Pkwy., opposite Sunset Elementary School, just before the road passes under I–90.
- 9.0 Timberlake Public Park is to the left.
- 11.4 Lake Sammamish State Park entrance to left.
- 12.0 Turn left on E. Lake Sammamish Pkwy.
- 22.0 Left onto NE 65th St., just before crossing railroad tracks.
- 22.3 Continue straight into Marymoor Park, and follow road through park.
- 23.0 End back at velodrome.

39

Chilly Hilly Ramble

Winslow—Port Madison—Blakely Harbor—Winslow

The Chilly Hilly ride, held the last weekend in February, is tradition-ally the first major event of the bicycling season for Puget Sound area cyclists. Several thousand participants brave wet and cold weather to ride the 28-mile loop around Bainbridge Island, across Puget Sound from Seattle.

What's the attraction? First of all, the Chilly Hilly includes the fea-tures that make bicycling in this area so enjoyable: It starts with a ferry ride and then follows low-traffic roads along beautiful shore lands, through lush evergreen forests and friendly communities. Bain-bridge, like other islands, is hilly; completing this ride is challenging enough to let you feel proud of your accomplishment.

Riding with a couple of thousand other enthusiasts makes it extra fun. Bicyclists take over the ferries, replacing the business suits and briefcases of weekday commuters with the Lycra suits and lightweight bicycles of weekend adventurers. It's a friendly, sociable event offering a chance to meet riders from all over the region.

With the right gear bicycling the Chilly Hilly can be pleasant even under the worst conditions. Wear tights over your bicycling shorts and a good rain jacket or windbreaker. If the weather is cold, use long-fingered gloves, wool socks, and a knit hat or ear warmer under your helmet. If in doubt take along an extra sweater. Be prepared for hills and steep descents.

The ride begins at the Winslow ferry terminal in Eagle Harbor. Winslow is a friendly town, part tourist destination, part commuter stop, and the commercial center for the Bainbridge Island community. From town the route goes north over mild hills along the island's eastern shore. At the northeast corner you pass Fay Bainbridge State Park, a pleasant place to stop to rest, picnic, or walk the beach. You'll continue counterclockwise around Bainbridge, past Port Madison, the first European settlement on the island (seventeen white residents in 1857) and across busy Highway 305. From there the hills seem to get progressively higher and closer together. Try to develop speed on the descents to give yourself a start up the next hill.

Children and civic organizations set up cider and cookie stops along the Chilly Hilly route. Hot cider really hits the spot while bicycling on a cold February morning. If you ride this route during summer or autumn, you may find produce sold at small roadside stands, including the island's most popular traditional product, strawberries.

At Bainbridge's southern end you pass the turnoff to Fort Ward State Park. The fort once housed large artillery guns, antisubmarine defenses, and military communications equipment. It's now a peaceful picnic site and public beach. Farther around the corner you pass Blakely Harbor. During the late 1800s it was one of the biggest mill towns and shipbuilding centers on the west coast. Once crowded with tall ships waiting to be filled with lumber and sail all over the Pacific Ocean, Port Blakely is now a quiet residential community.

The ride ends by circling Eagle Harbor. There is a last big climb, and you won't be alone if you choose to dismount and walk. Once in Winslow you can reward yourself at any of a number of stores, cafés, and candy shops. Riders often enjoy a hearty lunch in Winslow before returning to Seattle. The ferry ride back from Chilly Hilly is your chance to commiserate with other wet and tired bicyclists. The worse the weather the more you'll enjoy these breaks.

The Basics

Start: Winslow ferry dock on Bainbridge Island. Take the Winslow ferry from Pier 52 in Seattle.
Length: 28 miles.
Terrain: Hilly, mostly rural roads.

Food: Stores and restaurants in Winslow; convenience stores at 4.5, 16.8, and 19.8 miles.

For more information: Cascade Bicycle Club, P.O. Box 31299, Seattle, WA 98103; (206) 522–BIKE. Bainbridge Island Chamber of Commerce, 153 Madrone Lane N., Bainbridge Island, WA 98110; (206) 842–3700.

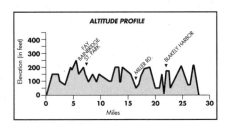

Miles & Directions

- 0.0 From the ferry terminal, follow Olympic Dr. At the top of the hill turn right on Winslow Way. At the far side of town, turn left on Ferncliff Ave. Follow Ferncliff as it curves left.
- 2.5 Turn right on Moran Rd.
- 2.8 Turn right on Maniton Beach Dr. Bear right in a few yards at fork to stay on Maniton. Ride along beach.
- 4.1 Follow curve left onto Valley Rd., then turn right at a small group of shops called "the Village," on Sunrise Dr.
- 7.2 Just past Fay Bainbridge State Park turn left onto Lafayette Ave.
- 7.8 Turn left on Euclid Ave., then left again on Phelps.
- 8.6 Turn right onto Hidden Cove Rd.
- 10.2 Cross Hwy. 305.
- 10.6 Turn left onto Manzanita Rd.
- 11.9 Turn right on Peterson Hill Rd.
- 12.4 Turn right on Miller Rd.
- 12.9 Turn right on Arrow Pt. Dr., and continue as it curves left.
- 13.8 Follow road as it curves right. Pass Battle Pt. Park.
- 14.1 Turn left on Frey Ave., then left again on Battle Pt. Dr.

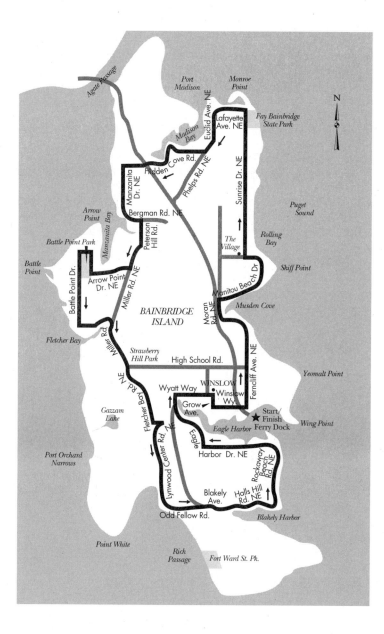

- 16.4 Turn right on Miller Rd., toward Lynwood.
- 17.1 Island Center Park and Community Center.
- 18.8 Turn right on Lynwood Center Rd.
- 20.5 Bear left onto Odd Fellow Rd.
- 21.1 Bear right at stop sign onto Halls Hill Rd.
- 22.4 Ride carefully as you take a sharp left curve at bottom of a steep descent onto Rockaway Beach Rd.
- 23.0 Follow curve left to Eagle Harbor Dr.
- 26.1 Turn right at stop sign onto busy Blakely Ave. Follow the road as it curves right onto Wyatt Ave.
- 26.9 Turn right at top of hill on Grow Ave., then follow the road left onto Winslow, where you can enjoy a wide selection of stores and restaurants. Turn right on Olympic Dr. to ferry terminal.
- 28.0 End.

40

Mount Si Ramble

Snoqualmie—Mount Si—North Bend—Snoqualmie

This loop through the upper Snoqualmie Valley is based on the shorter Snoqualmie Bicycle Century route. It is a relatively easy and very enjoyable ride through forest-covered hills, valley bottomlands, and the town of North Bend.

The route follows Mill Pond Road along the Snoqualmie River, then proceeds onto Tokul Road through timber-covered hills. You'll follow the road as it curves onto 53rd Way and descend past a large lumber mill, back down to the Snoqualmie River. You pass through the historic Reinig Sycamore Corridor, two rows of beautiful trees planted in 1929 that lined the main street of what once was Snoqualmie Falls, a town that no longer exists.

Straight ahead are the towering cliffs of Mount Si. The mountain, named after settler Josiah "Si" Meritt, is a western outpost of the Cascade Mountains, as indicated by its solid rock faces. Ride almost to the base of the mountain, then turn onto 428th Avenue to cross the North and Middle forks of the Snoqualmie River and into North Bend. You may want to take time to explore this town. The Snoqualmie Valley Historical Museum at 320 North Bend Boulevard includes Native American, pioneer, farming, and logging exhibits. It's just down the street from the Mar-T Café (famous as the "RR Café" in the *Twin Peaks* television program).

The route back to Snoqualmie on Boalch Avenue crosses the flat valley land that was the thousand-acre Borst Hop Farm, once the largest hop farm in the world. This farm was a major employer in the region, attracting hundreds of harvest workers each year.

Older residents still tell stories about the festive camps where workers danced to fiddle and guitar music on late autumn nights after picking hops all day long. Insect infestations killed the hop plants early in this century. Now the land is a golf course and residential developments. It's an easy ride back to the Snoqualmie City Hall. Just down the street you can celebrate your return with gourmet ice cream at Debbie's Soda Shoppe.

The Basics

Start: Snoqualmie City Hall, at corner of River and Railroad Ave. Take exit 27 from I–90, and follow signs to Snoqualmie. Turn left at flashing light onto Railroad Ave.
Length: 13.7 miles.
Terrain: Moderately hilly ride on rural roads.
Food: Restaurants and stores in North Bend, at 10 miles.
For more information: North Bend Chamber of Commerce, P.O. Box 357, North Bend, WA 98045; (206) 888–1678.

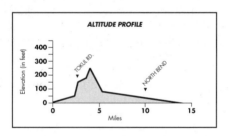

Miles & Directions

- 0.0 Go south on Falls Ave. 1 block, turn left on Newton St., go 1 block, then right onto Park Ave.
- 0.6 Turn left onto Meadowbrook Way. Cross the Snoqualmie River, then turn left on Mill Pond Rd.

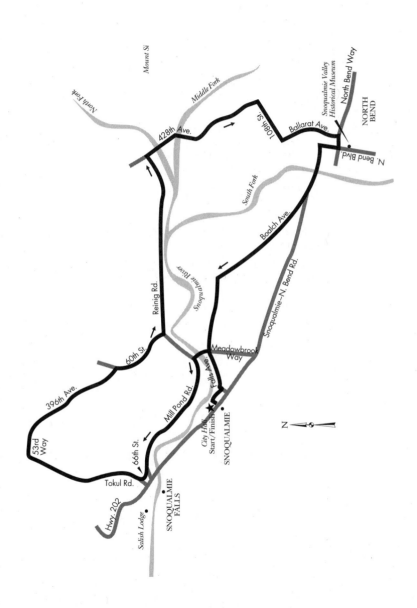

- 2.2 Bear right onto 66th St. Go up a short hill, then turn right onto Tokul Rd., which continues a short but steep climb.
- 3.6 Bear right onto 53rd Way.
- 4.0 Continue straight onto 396th Ave.
- 4.4 Merge right onto SE 60th St.
- 5.7 Turn left onto Reinig Rd., proceed through the Reinig Sycamore Corridor, and along the Snoqualmie River. Ride toward the towering cliffs of Mount Si.
- 7.5 Turn right on 428th Ave. SE.
- 9.0 Follow the road through the outskirts of North Bend as it curves right onto 108th St., and then left onto Ballarat Ave.
- 10.0 Turn right onto North Bend Way, through downtown.
- 10.2 Turn right at light onto North Bend Blvd. Follow the road as it curves left toward Hwy. 202 and crosses over the South Fork of the Snoqualmie River.
- 11.0 Turn right onto Boalch Ave.
- 13.0 Cross Meadowbrook Way; the road becomes Park Ave.
- 13.4 Bear left onto Newton St. Go 1 block, turn right onto Falls Ave.
- 13.7 End back at Snoqualmie City Hall.

41

Vashon Island Ramble

*Vashon Ferry Dock—Wax Orchards—Burton
Dockton—Vashon Center—Vashon Ferry Dock*

Vashon Island sits in Puget Sound, accessible by a short ferry ride from both Seattle and Tacoma. This location and its many miles of rural roads make it a popular destination for day rides. Vashon is a fun place to bicycle. Around practically every corner you'll encounter spectacular views of Puget Sound, Mount Rainier, or the skylines of Seattle or Tacoma. Along the way you'll see beautiful homes built during the island's early days and small homesteads. Islanders are proud of their locally produced food specialties, including tofu, baked goods, and abundant fresh-grown produce in season. What more could a bicyclist want?

Vashon's busiest bicycling day is the annual Ride Around Vashon Island (RAVI), sponsored by the Vashon Rotary Club and the Alki Bicycle Club of Seattle. It attracts bicyclists from all over the region and motivates many island residents to pump up the tires on their own bikes to enjoy a day of riding. The RAVI route, presented here, offers many highlights: snacks from the Wax Orchards gourmet natural fruit products, visits to the lovely historic towns of Burton and Dockton, lunch at Sound Foods restaurant and bakery, rides along miles of beautiful waterfront roads, and, of course, ferry rides to and from the island. There is something for everybody: from beginners, who walk up the hills, to racers who ride multiple loops of the island in a single afternoon.

Vashon Island was named after Capt. James Vashon by his

friend Capt. George Vancouver, who first sighted the island in 1792. During the late 1800s Vashon Island was a major stopping point for the many small "Mosquito Fleet" steamships that plied Puget Sound. The island developed, first with small homesteads and small waterfront communities. Later a college was established at Burton and a drydock at Dockton, making Vashon a leading urban center at the turn of the century. But the arrival of railroads to the region gave mainland cities a major advantage and allowed island communities to settle into a slower pace. Although many residents now commute to work on the mainland, islanders still pride themselves on their friendly, rural lifestyle.

The ride as presented here starts at the north-end ferry terminal for Seattle-area bicyclists. Riders arriving from Tacoma start at the Tahlequah ferry dock on Vashon's southern tip, adding 4 miles to their distance. The route includes optional loops onto Jensen Point and Maury Island, both of which attach to Vashon by narrow isthmuses.

Like all of the Puget Sound islands, Vashon is hilly, with challenging climbs from each of the ferry docks. Out of courtesy it is usually best to wait for motor traffic to pass before starting up from the dock. This prevents bicyclists from delaying automobiles and allows you a chance to ride or walk up the first hill without the noise and exhaust of cars.

The Basics

Start: Vashon Island's north ferry dock. Take the Vashon Ferry from Fauntleroy in west Seattle. The alternative starting point is the Tahlequah ferry dock to the south. Take the ferry from Pt. Defiance in Tacoma. Either crossing takes about fifteen minutes.
Length: 28.4 or 42 miles.
Terrain: The island is hilly. Traffic is generally light to moderate on these rural roads except when ferries arrive.
Food: The Wax Orchards' gourmet fruit products specialty shop, at 9.8 miles, and the Sound Foods restaurant and bakery, at 35.4 miles, are favorites with bicyclists. There are grocery stores in Bur-

ton, at 16.5 miles; in Dockton at 23.2 miles; and in the town of Vashon, at 37.5 miles.

For more information: Vashon Chamber of Commerce, P.O. Box 1035, Vashon Island, WA 98070; (206) 463–6217. For RAVI information contact Alki Bicycle Club, 2611 California Ave. SW, Seattle, WA 98116; (206) 938–3322.

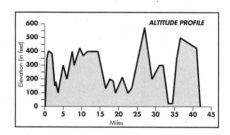

Miles & Directions

- 0.0 Ride or walk straight up 103rd Ave.
- 0.5 Turn right onto Vashon Island Hwy.
- 1.7 Bear right onto SW Cedarhurst Rd. Follow this road as it curves and winds down the shoreline and becomes 123rd Ave.
- 4.8 Turn right onto Westside Hwy. SW.
- 6.0 Follow the Westside Hwy. as it curves left.
- 8.0 Turn right at stop sign to stay on the Westside Hwy.
- 9.8 Turn right at 220th Ave. and follow curve left onto Wax Orchard Rd. SW.
- 10.5 Wax Orchards gourmet fruit products shop.
- 13.5 Turn left onto Vashon Hwy. to continue loop, or right for the ferry to Tacoma.
- 14.5 Inspiration Pt.
- 16.5 Village of Burton.

For an enjoyable 3-mile loop, turn right here onto SW Burton Dr., around Jensen Pt. to Burton Acres County Park.

- 17.5 Cross Judd Creek, then turn right onto Quartermaster Dr.

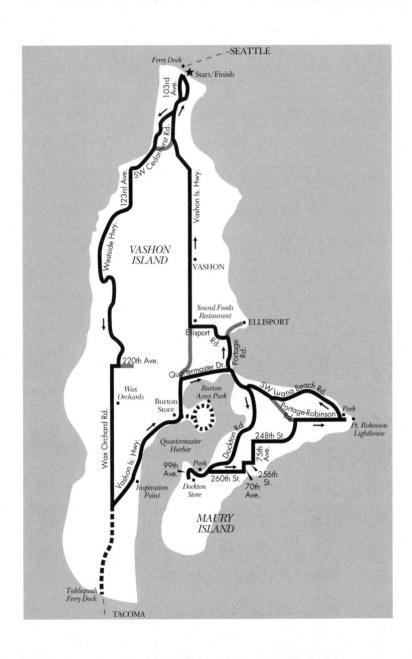

- 18.1 Ride along the narrow neck of land between Vashon and Maury islands.
- 19.1 Turn right onto Dockton Rd. SW, which takes you onto Maury Island.

For a shorter ride, turn left onto Portage Rd. and continue instructions at 32.7 miles.

- 20.1 Follow the road as it curves right.
- 22.8 Continue on Dockton Rd., then turn left as it becomes 99th Ave.
- 23.2 Turn around at Dockton General Store, west on 99th Ave. and right onto Dockton Rd.
- 24.1 Just past Dockton Park, turn right onto 260th St.
- 25.1 Turn left onto 70th Ave.
- 25.3 Follow road right onto SW 256th St.
- 25.6 Turn left onto 75th Ave. SW.
- 26.1 Turn right onto 248th St.
- 27.1 Follow the road as it curves left.
- 27.6 Turn right onto SW Pt. Robinson Rd.
- 28.8 Turn right to continue on Pt. Robinson Rd. This takes you to Pt. Robinson lighthouse and county park. From the park, turn around to ride back on Pt. Robinson Rd.
- 29.4 Continue straight onto SW Luana Beach Rd. Ride carefully; this is a narrow, winding road.
- 31.9 Turn right onto Portage-Robinson Rd.
- 32.7 Continue straight at stop sign onto Portage Rd.
- 33.4 Pass store.
- 34.2 Turn left onto Ellisport Rd.
- 35.4 Turn right onto Vashon Hwy. Sound Foods Restaurant and Bakery is at the corner.
- 37.5 Ride through the town of Vashon.
- 41.0 Follow Vashon Hwy. as it curves right.
- 42.0 End at ferry dock.

42

Lake Tapps Challenge

Orting—Burnett—Buckley
Lake Tapps—Puyallup Valley—Orting

This is the second loop offered each spring by the Tacoma Wheelmen as part of the Daffodil Classic ride. It is a popular ride in its own right, especially with local racers. The route follows some attractive low-traffic rural roads and includes a stop at Lake Tapps County Park, where you can enjoy a refreshing swim. It is an intermediate level ride, slightly more difficult than the southern loop, but well worth the effort.

The Daffodil Classic is one of the first major bicycle events of the season. Many participants are still a little out of shape, but they are full of enthusiasm, particularly if they are lucky enough to have a sparkling spring day. Bicyclists travel from all over the Puget Sound region to enjoy the ride and socialize with members of other bike clubs.

The ride begins like its companion route, the Daffodil Cruise, heading south on Highway 162. Follow the Carbon River as it curves north, past the Puyallup Fish Hatchery, and then onto South Pioneer Way, an old farm road that follows the valley's side. There is a little climbing, some good views, and little traffic. The road changes names as it meanders through the small community of South Prairie and up Tubbs Hill. Turn left onto Carbonado–South Prairie Road just before the town of Wilkeson (if you reach the old cemetery you've passed the turnoff), and follow Highway 162, Mundy Loss Road, and 112th Street through prairie lands to the community of Buckley.

Buckley sits at the base of the Cascade Mountains. The route goes right to the forest's edge, then circles back on Main Street through this friendly little town. Buckley still retains some of its turn-of-the-century charm. Local merchants welcome the small groups of colorfully dressed bicyclists who stock up on treats. A community park offers bicyclists a place to rest. On the other side of town the route follows the Old Sumner–Buckley Highway. It now carries only local traffic and not much of that. You'll have to dodge potholes, but most bicyclists enjoy the quiet environment and overgrown feel of this somewhat neglected old road. Follow the White River northwest toward Lake Tapps.

The lake's shore is lined with houses and private boat docks. Lake Tapps is a popular waterskiing course. The Tacoma Wheelmen use the Lake Tapps County Park at the lake's north end as a rest stop and checkpoint. A snack shop at the lake sells a limited selection of food, and on hot days bicyclists often stop for a refreshing swim.

The route continues to circle around Lake Tapps, flies down a 650-foot descent into the Puyallup Valley, then follows Riverside Drive and McCutcheon Road along the Puyallup River. Halfway up McCutcheon Road you will be rewarded with a view of the colorful valley and the curving Puyallup River. Descending to the bottom of the hill, you turn to cross the Puyallup River and join Highway 162 for the final leg back into Orting. Upon return you'll find the Orting City Park busy with tired but happy bicyclists celebrating their accomplishments.

The Basics

Start: Orting City Park, in the center of town. To get to Orting from the north, take Hwy. 167 to Sumner, go east on 410, then south on 162. From the south take I–5 to Hwy. 512 going east. Exit onto Pioneer Ave. in Puyallup. Take it to Hwy. 162 going south. Hwy. 162 passes Orting City Park.
Length: 45.5 miles.
Terrain: Moderately hilly.

Food: Stores and restaurants in Buckley, at 20 miles; convenience stores at 12.5, 31.5, 34, 36.5, and 41.5 miles; and the Lake Tapps Golf Course Café, at 28.6 miles.

For more information: Pierce County Parks Department, 9112 Lakewood Dr., S.W., Tacoma, WA 98499; (206) 593–4176. Bicycling map available.

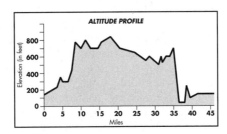

Miles & Directions

- 0.0 Start at Orting City Park. Head south on Washington St., which is also Hwy. 162. Follow Hwy. 162 as it zigzags past the big white Odd Fellows hall and out of town.
- 1.4 Bear left to stay on Hwy. 162.
- 3.8 Just after crossing over the Carbon River, turn right onto Pioneer Way, an enjoyable side road.
- 7.8 Turn right on 3rd Ave., which soon becomes Tubbs Rd.
- 11.3 Turn left on Carbonado–S. Prairie Rd. The intersection is not well marked; a sign simply says "Johns Rd." If you pass the old Wilkeson cemetery, you've missed the turnoff.
- 11.8 Continue straight at stop sign into Hwy. 165. You soon pass through Burnett, a one-store town.
- 13.5 Turn left at fork onto Hwy. 162 toward S. Prairie. Immediately cross over Spiketon Creek, then turn right onto Mundy Loss Rd., indicated by a WHITE RIVER MIDDLE SCHOOL sign.
- 14.8 Turn right onto 112th St. E.
- 15.8 Turn right at the first stop sign onto Ryan Rd., toward the

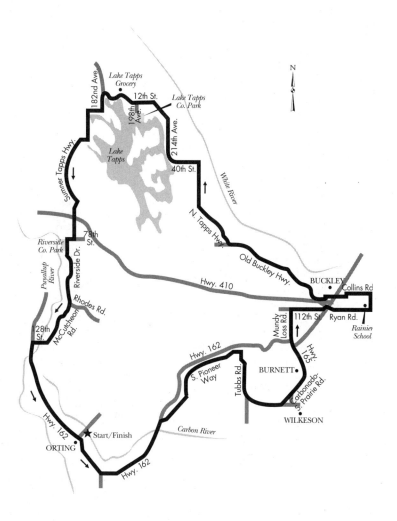

Rainier School. This immediately takes a slight jag, then straightens out to head east.

- 18.0 Turn left onto Levesque Rd. at the Rainier School.
- 18.5 Turn left onto Collins Rd. Follow this road past the Washington State University Agriculture Station and into the town of Buckley, where it becomes Main St.
- 20.3 Cross Hwy. 410.
- 20.5 When the road ends at a T, turn left onto Naches St. Turn right in 1 block at Mason Ave. This is the Old Sumner–Buckley Highway.
- 22.2 Turn right to stay on the highway.
- 24.5 Turn right onto the Buckley-Tapps Hwy. E. The White River Valley is to your right.
- 27.5 Follow the road left onto 40th St.
- 28.4 Follow the road right onto 214th Ave. Lake Tapps is on your left. You can stop for a snack at the Lake Tapps Golf Course Coffee Shop. This road curves left to become 12th St.
- 31.0 To visit Lake Tapps County Park, turn left on 198th Ave. E.
- 31.5 Lake Tapps Grocery and Café.
- 32.0 Turn left onto 182nd Ave. E., the Sumner-Tapps Hwy.
- 34.8 Begin a long and steep descent into the Puyallup Valley. Check your brakes!
- 36.5 Continue straight under the Hwy. 410 bridge.
- 37.3 Turn right onto 78th St., and in a short distance turn left onto Riverside Dr. E. The Puyallup River is on the right.
- 38.8 Turn left onto McCutcheon Rd. The road zigzags, then a short hill.
- 39.8 Turn right at Rhodes Rd. to stay on McCutcheon.
- 41.0 Cross bridge over the Puyallup River onto 128th St.
- 41.5 Turn left onto Hwy. 162.
- 45.5 End at park in downtown Orting.

43

Daffodil Cruise

Orting—Kapowsin—Ohop Valley—
Kapowsin—Orting

Before the turn of the century, the Tacoma Wheelmen Bicycle Club (founded in the 1880s) sponsored rides, races, and social events for the enjoyment of its members and bicyclists from all over the region. It still does. Early each spring the Tacoma Wheelmen sponsors the Daffodil Classic along country roads south and east of Tacoma. As one of the first club rides of the season, it draws eager club bicyclists from all over the Puget Sound region.

The ride begins in the town of Orting, a farming community 20 miles southeast of Tacoma. Participants have three choices: The south route has a short, 20-mile loop to Kapowsin and a longer 50-mile ride that continues south to the Ohop Valley. A second 50-mile loop north of Orting creates a full century ride.

The Daffodil is a spectacular ride, whatever combination of these routes you choose. The name comes from the acres of daffodil farms and other springtime blossoms that decorate the roadsides. Riders are surrounded by brilliant flowers, pastures, and forests. Looming majestically above the horizon is Mount Rainier, the highest peak in the Pacific Northwest. Rainier's glacier-covered cone is 25 miles away, but it looks close enough to touch with an outstretched arm.

This is the southern route, an enjoyable adventure through the farms, lakes, and forests of rural Pierce County. Traffic on most of these roads is light, and riders will find plenty of opportunities to stop for a snack or rest. After leaving Orting this route follows the Puyallup River Valley, past numerous small farms, ranches, and lumber mills, to Lake Kapowsin, a popular fishing spot. On a clear day you can use Mount Rainier to navigate. The mountain towers like a beacon straight ahead for the first 10 miles, to Lake Kapowsin.

Just past the lake the shorter route circles back to Orting. The longer route continues south into the Ohop Valley, approaching ever closer to the base of Mount Rainier. You'll pass Ohop Lake, where cyclists traditionally stop for a refreshing refill of water right out of a natural spring. The Ohop Valley is full of rolling hills covered with alternating forests and farms. For a few miles the ride follows the relatively busy Highway 161 past the Pioneer Farm Museum, then turns onto lower-traffic roads to complete the final stretch back to Kapowsin. In Kapowsin you will find the Kapowsin Store, Kapowsin Tavern, Kapowsin Post Office, and Kapowsin Grange.

The final 10 miles on the Orting-Kapowsin Highway is a pleasant ride with glimpses of farm life, forest-covered hills, and a scattering of country stores. Two miles from Orting you'll enjoy an exhilarating descent into the Puyallup River Valley and back to town. With routes like these it is no surprise that bicyclists have enjoyed themselves on these roads for more than a century. In another hundred years the Tacoma Wheelmen will probably still sponsor the delightful Daffodil Classic.

The Basics

Start: Orting City Park, in the center of town. Take Hwy. 167 from the north, or I–5 to Hwy. 512 from the south, to Puyallup. From Puyallup take Hwy. 162 south to Orting. Hwy. 162 passes the Orting City Park.

Length: 20 or 51 miles. Combined with the nearly 50-mile Lake Tapps Challenge described next, the two create a century ride.

Terrain: Rolling hills. The only steep incline is the final descent into Orting.

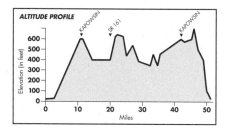

Food: Several choices in Orting; a store and tavern in Kapowsin; a store at mile 35, at the intersection with Hwy. 7; and two stores on the final stretch between Kapowsin and Orting.

For more information: Tacoma Wheelmen Bicycle Club, P.O. Box 112078, Tacoma, WA 98411; (206) 759–2800.

Miles & Directions

- 0.0 Start at Orting City Park, in the center of Orting. Head south on Washington St., which is also Hwy. 162.
- 0.2 Zigzag on Hwy. 162 as it passes the big white Odd Fellows Hall, and out of town.
- 1.3 Turn right onto Orville Rd. You will see the Crocker Grange building at the far corner of the intersection.
- 4.7 Bear right and cross the Puyallup River bridge.
- 10.7 You are now in Kapowsin.

For the 20-mile loop, turn right onto the Orting-Kapowsin Hwy., and follow instructions from mile 41.0.

For the 50-mile loop, turn left onto Orville Rd. E. Follow this road past Kapowsin and Ohop lakes, into the Ohop Valley.

- 18.5 Here you should find a natural spring fountain coming out of the hillside next to the roadway. A boat launch 0.5 mile farther down the road has public toilets.

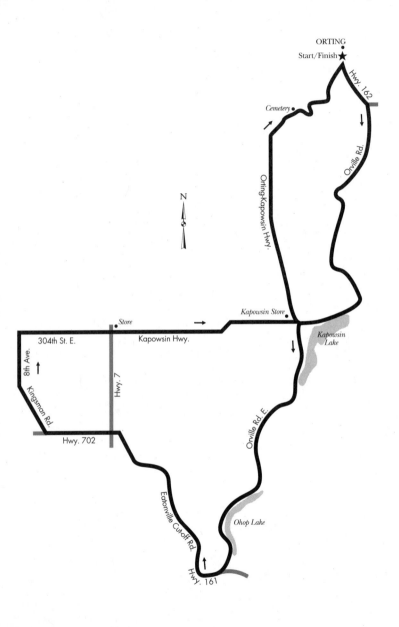

ORTING

Start/Finish

Hwy. 162

Cemetery

Orville Rd.

Orting-Kapowsin Hwy.

N

Kapowsin Store

Kapowsin Lake

Store

304th St. E.

Kapowsin Hwy.

8th Ave.

Hwy. 7

Orville Rd. E.

Kingsmon Rd.

Hwy. 702

Eatonville Cut-off Rd.

Ohop Lake

Hwy. 161

- 20.0 Turn right onto Hwy. 161. This is the busiest stretch of roadway on this route. Fortunately it has a good, wide shoulder.
- 21.6 Dogwood Park, at the side of the road.
- 21.7 Turn left onto Eatonville Cut-off Rd.
- 26.5 Continue straight across Hwy. 7. You are now on Hwy. 702 going west.
- 28.7 Turn right onto Kinsman Rd.
- 30.8 Continue on the road, which is now called 8th Ave. E.
- 32.0 Turn right onto 304th St. E.
- 35.1 Continue straight across Hwy. 7. There is a Qwik Mart and tavern at this corner. You are now on the Kapowsin Hwy.
- 41.0 You are now back in Kapowsin. Turn left onto the Orting-Kapowsin Hwy.
- 42.0 Rough railroad track just past the OK Country Store. Cross with care.
- 49.0 Just past the Orting cemetery, you encounter a steep 1-mile descent.
- 50.0 Follow the highway left. The Soldier's Home, founded in 1891 for retired military, is on your right.
- 50.5 Cross the Puyallup River. The road is now called Calistoga St.
- 51.0 Return to Orting City Park.

44

Wolf Haven Cruise

Millersylvania—Fort Lewis—Rainier
Wolf Haven—Tenino—Millersylvania

Bicycling rural Thurston County can be sheer pleasure: riding on winding roads through evergreen forests that are so quiet you hear the gurgling of small creeks and birds singing praise. On clear days sunlight sparkles through the canopy, creating myriad shades of green that dance in the slightest breeze. The forest offers the sweet aroma of cedar. In cool weather all is calm and muted. There's a timeless quality to the untamed lands that still cover much of this area.

At almost every curve you'll be delighted with a new view or a place to stop and explore. In the valleys you pass old homesteads, small farms with simple buildings constructed of locally cut lumber and shingles. These are remnants of the area's first white settlers, known as "stump farmers" because they often plowed around the largest stumps left in their fields after hand-clearing their land. It's easy to imagine what this region was like a century earlier when large animals, including wolves and cougars, roamed wild.

The Wolf Haven Cruise is one of four routes of different lengths offered as part of the Capital Bicycling Club's Wolf Haven Century, a fund-raiser held the third Sunday of September to support the Wolf Haven Wildlife Refuge. Each loop includes a stop at Wolf Haven, where riders rest, picnic, and visit this unique facility.

The rides begin at Millersylvania State Park. On summer days this pleasant lake-side park is filled with families picnicking, camping, and swimming. Classic log buildings, constructed during the depression by the Civilian Conservation Corps, are scattered among huge evergreen trees. If you have time, stretch your legs on a nature walk, or rent a boat at adjacent Deep Lake Resort.

Exiting the park you'll soon find the quiet solitude that makes bicycling such a pleasant way to experience this region. Most of this ride follows flat lowlands or mildly rolling hills, making use of well-maintained back roads with light traffic. You ride through alternating forest, meadows, and areas of scattered homes. You're likely to see more sheep, cows, and horses than people, especially if you ride on a weekend morning or midday during the week, when traffic is light. In 5 miles you pass the Country Cider Mill, a barn-turned-juice-factory. There you can fill your water bottles with apple and raspberry juice or purchase local produce in season.

If the day is clear, you will soon catch a view of Mount Rainier in the distance. It will keep you company for the rest of the ride, its beautiful snow-topped peak often visible over the trees. On Rainier Road you ride several miles through the Fort Lewis Military Reservation, a vast expanse of forests and prairie. You are unlikely to see any sign of the army, although soldiers do occasionally hold maneuvers in the area; the army requests that you stay on the roadway. Eventually you reach the small town of Rainier.

You now circle back northwestward on some of the most rural roads of this ride, for a visit to Wolf Haven. The refuge is a pleasant place to rest or picnic in the shade of evergreen trees. Don't be surprised if peacocks wander by or deer browse in the distance. Visiting the refuge you can't help but ponder how lucky we humans are to share our world with so many interesting and diverse species.

Wolf Haven is sanctuary to nearly three dozen wolves rescued from abuse or destruction. They now live comfortably and safely in large pens. Wolf Haven is staffed by volunteers and supported entirely by public contributions. During tours the dedicated staff describe the personalities of each wolf and share their extensive knowledge of wolf lore and current preservation issues. Although visitors must keep their distance, experienced staff members often enter the pens to wrestle with the playful wolves. The refuge is open daily from 10:00 A.M. to 5:00 P.M. Admission is $3.00 for adults, $2.00 for children.

A few miles past Wolf Haven you climb the biggest hill of the ride, then coast into the town of Tenino, a friendly community of twelve hundred people. Stop for a rest or to visit the antique shops lining the main street. You will notice that many of the buildings here are constructed of locally quarried Tenino Sandstone, a resource that once made this town famous.

Leaving the bustle of Tenino, the back roads over forest-covered hills are especially enjoyable. You may want to slow down to savor these last miles of quiet and undeveloped beauty. All too soon you turn onto busier Tilley Road, and back to Millersylvania Park. There you can relax by taking a cool swim in Deep Lake, or simply lean back against one of the giant trees and muse on the joys of your day.

The Basics

Start: Millersylvania State Park, on Tilley Rd. 10 miles south of Olympia. To get there from I-5, take the 93rd Ave. exit, go 1 mile east, then turn right onto Tilley Rd. Millersylvania Park is 3 miles south.

Length: 37.4 or 19.4 miles.

Terrain: Rural roads over rolling hills and flat valleys. Roads are well maintained, and the stretches of highway with heavy traffic have good shoulders.

Food: Stops include the Country Cider Mill, at 4.8 miles; a store and café in the town of Rainier, at 17.2 miles; J&M Saloon at 27.8 miles; and stores and cafés in Tenino, at 31 miles.

For more information: Capital Bicycling Club, P.O. Box 642, Olympia, WA 98507; (360) 956–3321. Wolf Haven, 3111 Offut Lake Rd., Tenino, WA 98589; (800) 448–WOLF.

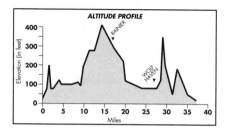

Miles & Directions

- 0.0 Turn left from Millersylvania State Park onto Tilley Rd.
- 1.0 Turn right onto 113th Ave.
- 2.2 Bear left at fork to stay on 113th Ave.
- 3.7 Turn left on Old 99.

For shorter option, turn right, go .5 mile, and turn left onto Waldrick Rd. After 2.2 miles turn right on Offut Lake Rd. Go 2.5 miles to Wolf Haven. Follow instructions from 26.9 miles below.

- 4.5 Turn right on Rich Rd. You soon pass the Country Cider Mill. Stay on Rich Rd. along its zigzag course.
- 6.4 Turn right on 89th Ave.
- 7.8 Bear right at intersection onto Fir Tree Rd.
- 8.5 Turn right on Rainier Rd. You soon enter the Fort Lewis Military Reservation.
- 13.8 Left onto Military Rd.
- 15.4 Turn right on Hubbard Rd.
- 16.9 Turn right on Binghampton, which is also Hwy. 507. Turn right, just past the Rainier Market, onto Minnesota, which becomes Rainier Rd.
- 17.9 Where Rainier Rd. curves right, continue straight onto 138th Ave.
- 19.4 Where 138th Ave. ends, turn left on Military Rd.
- 19.9 Turn right on Waldrick Rd.
- 24.3 After crossing the Deschutes River, turn left on Offut Lake Rd.

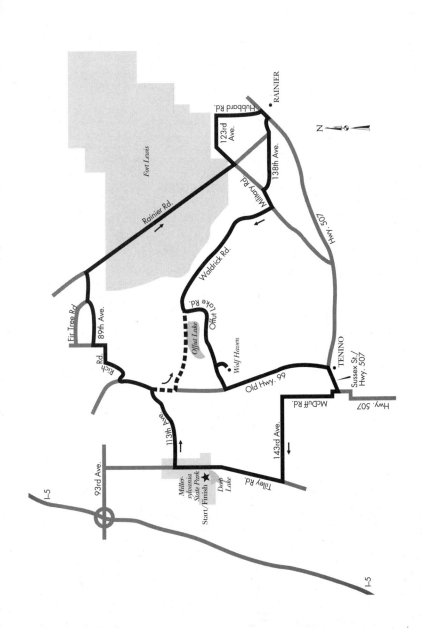

- 26.9 Wolf Haven driveway. To visit the sanctuary, follow signs 0.1 mile to the refuge's information center.
- 27.4 Turn left onto Old Hwy. 99. You will climb a 0.5-mile grade, then descend into Tenino.
- 30.5 Turn right on Sussex St., Tenino's main drag, which is also Hwy. 507.
- 31.1 Where Hwy. 507 curves left, turn right onto Wickman Rd. The road becomes McDuff Rd., and then 143rd Ave. No matter what it's called, it's a beautiful road with light traffic.
- 35.3 Turn right on Tilley Rd.
- 37.4 End back at Millersylvania Park.

45

Rainbow Falls Cruise

Rochester—Independence Valley
Adna—Rainbow Falls State Park

Outside of a few urbanized areas, the region between Puget Sound to the north and the Columbia River to the south is a lightly populated wonderland of forests, rivers, and small farms. Bicyclists can enjoy hundreds of miles of low-traffic roads through lush evergreen environments, with occasional stops in friendly communities.

The Rainbow Falls Cruise is an excellent example of the bicycling opportunities in this region. Every curve of this ride offers a delightful view. It starts in the small town of Rochester, travels south through Independence Valley, follows the Chehalis River, climbs Manners Hill, and meanders along Bunker Creek. You'll enjoy 24 miles of riding through beautiful forests and quiet farmlands before encountering a single store in the community of Adna. Traffic is so light you could almost nap on the roadway. From Adna the route follows Highway 6 along the Chehalis River to spectacular Rainbow Falls State Park, where riders can spend the night in hiker/ biker campsites. This is a traditional ride sponsored occasionally by the Capital Bicycling Club of Olympia.

An alternative route avoids civilization altogether, turning off the main road before Adna and climbing over Ceres Hill. This route, which includes a 5-mile stretch of gravel roads, provides a back-door entrance to Rainbow Falls Park. As gravel roads go, these are in good condition; we towed our infant son in a trailer behind a touring bicycle with 1¼-inch tires over these roads without problem. If you use this option, be sure to bring along sufficient food and water, as there are no stores or public services along the way, and there is nowhere to buy food at Rainbow Falls.

Much of the 124-acre Rainbow Falls State Park is covered with virgin forests of towering cedar, fir, and hemlock trees. During the Great Depression, the Civilian Conservation Corps constructed classic stone-and-log structures that visitors still enjoy. Park facilities include rest rooms with showers, covered kitchens, and a swimming hole in the river just below the beautiful falls. On hot days the riverbank is crowded with local children frolicking in the cool water. For more information on Rainbow Falls Park, call (206) 291–3767.

The Basics

Start: Downtown Rochester, in front of the Rochester Primary School. To get there by car, take I–5 about 15 miles south of Olympia, follow Hwy. 12 west 5 miles to Rochester. By bicycle from the Olympia area, take the Littlerock Rd. to Littlerock, then follow scenic Hwy. 121 south along the Black River to Rochester. Olympia to Rochester is approximately 17 miles.

Length: 36 miles each way by Hwy. 6, 31 miles over Ceres Hill.

Terrain: Most of the ride follows low-traffic roads through farm valleys, plus 12 miles of riding on the shoulder of Hwy. 6. The alternative route avoids traffic but requires 5 miles of gravel roads through forest-covered hills.

Food: Stores and restaurants in Rochester, at the beginning of the ride, and a small store in Adna, at mile 24. The alternative route over Ceres Hill has no services at all. There is no store at Rainbow Falls State Park, so bring sufficient supplies.

For more information: Rochester Chamber of Commerce, 10139 Hwy. 12 SW, Rochester, WA 98579; (360) 273–8013.

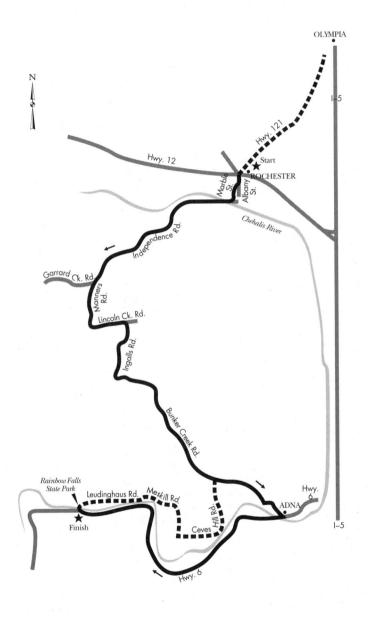

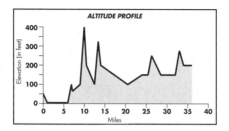

Miles & Directions

- 0.0 Ride south on Albany St., past the Broken Wheel Saloon.
- 0.3 Turn right at Swede Hall onto 185th Ave., then follow the road as it immediately curves left onto Marble St.
- 1.2 Turn right on Independence Rd.
- 8.5 Bear left at fork onto Manners Rd.
- 10.5 Turn left on Lincoln Creek Rd.
- 12.0 Turn right on Ingalls Rd.
- 14.0 Turn left on Bunker Creek Rd.

For the 31-mile option—

- Turn right onto Ceres Hill Rd. just after crossing a small creek at 20.5 miles. Much of Ceres Hill Rd. is gravel. Turn right on Meskill Rd. (2 miles of gravel), at 24.5 miles. Turn right onto Leudinghaus Rd., at 28.0 miles. End at Rainbow Falls State Park. To find the park's back entrance, look for a white wooden gate on the left side of the road with a NO PARKING sign, just past mailbox #600.
- 20.5 Continue straight. Follow Bunker Creek into Adna.
- 24.0 Turn right onto Hwy. 6. Adna Store is at intersection. Cross bridge over the Chehalis River.
- 36.0 End at Rainbow Falls State Park. Watch for signs to park entrance.

46

Lewis County
Historical Cruise

Chehalis—Centralia—Claquato
Pleasant Valley—Chehalis

The rural roads of Lewis County, with light traffic and beautiful scenery, are a bicyclist's paradise. Local bicyclists create endless combinations of routes, from flat and easy valley roads to challenging climbs through forest-covered hills. Bicyclists from all over southwest Washington congregate in Chehalis early each spring to enjoy the Broken Spokes Cycling Folks' Historical Lewis County Bicycle Ride, which highlights the best of these roads while visiting local historical sites.

The ride begins at the Lewis County Historical Museum. The old Chehalis train depot, a grand brick building constructed in 1912, is the museum's home. Touring the museum gives an overview of the region's history and traditional industries. A half mile from the museum, you pass through the Pennsylvania Historic District, 5 blocks of elaborate houses from the "carriage era." The area gives you a feeling for what this mill town was like before the turn of the century.

At 4.5 miles you ride over the new Chehalis River bridge. Adjacent to this is the site of the Old Hanging Bridge, where Wesley Everest, an I.W.W. organizer, was lynched after a clash with American Legion members on Armistice Day 1919. The conflict began when Legion members attacked the local I.W.W. office; four Legion members were shot and killed. Although eleven more "Wobblies" were punished for the legionnaires' deaths, nobody was prosecuted for the lynching. Local residents still argue over who was at fault in the "Centralia Massacre."

It's pleasant riding as you get out of the urban area into farms, pastures, and woodlands. At 10.5 miles you pass the site of the once growing community of Claquato (Chehalis Indian for "High Ground"). The town died after being bypassed by the railroad during the late 1800s. The little Claquato Church, built in 1859, is the oldest Protestant church in Washington.

You ride for 8 miles farther on the well-named Pleasant Valley Road. The Mustard Seed restaurant at mile 28 is a popular lunch stop for bicyclists, so the staff is accustomed to our big appetites and flashy clothes. It's a few miles farther east on Avery Road to the Jackson Highway.

The 1-mile ride to the Jackson Prairie Courthouse is a must-see detour for anyone interested in local history. This small building, constructed in 1845, served as U.S. District Court, post office, and store for more than fifty years when it was home to John and Matilda Jackson and their six children. The Jackson family welcomed many arrivals to Washington and provided hospitality to travelers.

Turn south on the Jackson Highway, pass the Matilda Jackson Park, a tract of land donated to the state by the Jackson family. The park's towering evergreen trees provide a glimpse of what this area must have been like for the first settlers, before the ancient forests were cut. Starting as a dirt path and later developing into Highway 99, the Jackson Highway served as a major connection between the Columbia River and Puget Sound. Since I–5 now carries most traffic, old gas stations, stores, and motels along the Jackson Highway have been converted to other uses.

You'll ride down the Jackson Highway for almost 5 miles, then complete your return to Chehalis on a series of small roads that follow closely to I–5. The last mile is a tour of Chehalis, from the McKinley Stump (President Theodore Roosevelt, standing on this stump, addressed ten thousand people in 1903), through residential neighborhoods, to the city's historic downtown, and back to the County Historical Museum. You will surely agree that it has been a delightful and fascinating ride through the countryside and history of Lewis County.

The Basics

Start: Lewis County Historical Museum, housed in the old train depot in downtown Chehalis. To drive there exit I–5 in Chehalis, turn right on National Ave., and follow signs to museum.
Length: 17 or 43.8 miles.
Terrain: Mostly flat roads, light traffic, and a few hills.
Food: Adna Store, at 15 miles; restaurants and stores at 28.1 miles; Mary's Corner Market, at 31 miles; stores and restaurants at 38.2 miles.
For more information: Broken Spokes Cycling Folks, 414 W. Pear St., Centralia, WA 98531.

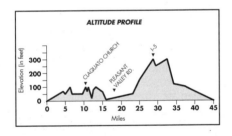

Miles & Directions

- 0.0 Exiting the museum parking lot, turn left on West St. Cross three sets of railroad tracks, take the first left onto State St.
- 0.3 Turn right onto Prindle St. In 1 block follow it as it curves right onto St. Helens Ave., then take another right onto Pennsylvania Ave., through the historic Pennsylvania District.

- 0.6 Turn left on West St. In a few blocks you will cross over I–5. On the other side of the bridge, follow the road as it curves left to become Airport Rd.
- 3.1 Pass Hamilton Farms sign, follow road parallel to the freeway, to the outskirts of Centralia.
- 4.6 Turn left on Mellen St. Cross the Chehalis River at the site of the Old Hanging Bridge.
- 4.8 Bear right onto Cooks Hill Rd.
- 5.2 Turn left on Schueber Rd., and continue past jog onto Old Military Rd.
- 10.3 Right onto Hwy. 6.
- 10.5 Turn right at Chilvers Rd., then immediately left on Stearns Rd. and again onto Claquato Rd., past the Claquato historic site sign. Follow Claquato Rd. up the hill.
- 10.7 Turn left onto Elm View Ave.
- 11.0 Pass the 1859 Claquato Church.
- 11.1 Turn left at stop sign on Stearn Rd. Pass Pioneer Cemetery on your right.

For the 17-mile ride, turn right here. At the bottom of the hill, turn right then immediate left onto Hwy. 6. Cross the Chehalis River and I–5 into the town of Chehalis, where road becomes Main St. Turn left on Cascade Ave.; in 3 blocks turn left at stop sign onto Market St. This takes you through downtown Chehalis back to your start.

- 12.0 Turn right onto Laughlin Rd.
- 13.0 Left at stop sign onto Chilvers Rd.
- 13.9 Turn left onto Dieckman Rd.
- 14.7 Pass Adna High School.
- 15.0 Enter Adna.
- 15.2 Turn left at stop sign onto Bunker Creek Rd. Pass Adna store to right.
- 15.4 Turn right onto Hwy. 6, cross the Chehalis River.
- 15.6 Turn left on Twin Oaks Rd.
- 17.1 Turn right onto Pleasant Valley Rd.
- 25.2 Turn left onto Hwy. 603.
- 25.4 Turn right onto Avery Rd., and cross railroad tracks.
- 28.1 Cross I–5; road becomes Hwy. 12. Restaurants and stores.

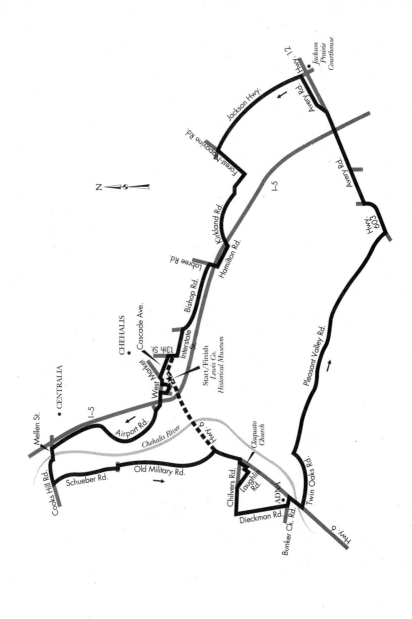

- 28.8 Turn left onto Avery Rd.
- 30.8 Turn left onto Jackson Hwy. Pass the Matilda Jackson State Park in 0.2 mile. Turn right for a .5-mile detour to the Jackson Prairie Courthouse historical site.
- 34.7 Turn left on Forest Napavine Rd.
- 35.8 Turn right on Kirkland Rd.
- 38.2 Turn left, opposite the Rib Eye Restaurant, onto Rush Rd., to pass under I–5. At the stop sign on the other side, turn right onto Hamilton Rd. and follow it parallel to I–5.
- 40.2 Turn right on Labree Rd. Cross over I–5.
- 40.6 Turn left at stop sign onto Bishop Rd.
- 41.4 Turn left onto Interstate St., just before railroad tracks.
- 42.5 Turn right on Parkland Dr., which soon curves left to become 13th St.
- 42.8 Turn left on William St., the first left past city park. Follow William St. as it curves right onto Cascade Ave.
- 43.8 Turn left onto Market St. at stop sign. Follow Market through downtown Chehalis, back to Lewis County Historical Museum.

47

St. Helens Challenge

Iron Creek—Bear Meadow—Meta Lake—Iron Creek

The eruption of Mount St. Helens on May 18, 1980, was one of the most dramatic geologic events in recent Northwest history. In the course of a few seconds, the mountain's upper quarter exploded with sufficient force to catapult rocks and trees into the air and blew a plume of volcanic ash hundreds of miles across the state. In that moment the mountain's forests, rivers, and glaciers were transformed into charred logs, mud slides, and dust.

The St. Helens National Volcanic Monument makes an excellent bicycling destination. Described here is a favorite route used by the Bicycle Adventures Company, which leads luxury bicycle tours around the Pacific Northwest. It is a dramatic ride that contrasts lush evergreen forests with the stark landscape of the blast area. This is a "don't miss" experience for strong riders who enjoy long climbs. Due to heavy weekend tourist traffic, you may prefer to ride off-season or on a weekday. If possible start early in the day before traffic and temperatures rise.

The most common approach for this ride is through the town of Randle, on Highway 12. Stock up on food in Randle since services along the route are limited. The ride begins at the Iron Creek Campground on the bank of the Cispus River. Follow Route 25, one of the main access highways through the Gifford Pinchot National Forest. It's a steady climb up the beautiful forested mountainside, with plenty of rewarding views and places to stop for a rest. After 10 miles of climbing—a 1,700-foot rise—you turn onto Route 99, with another 1,100 feet of ascent, to the Bear Meadow Interpretive Center. It's breathtaking, both because of the altitude and because you can see the impact of the volcanic eruption. Forests, once as tall and lush as what you just passed through, are now flattened.

As a bicyclist you have the advantage of being immersed in the visual drama that unfolds during your ride past the mountain. Take time to stop, perhaps in silent reverence at the power of the volcanic eruption and the perseverance of living things growing out of the ash. There are numerous vistas along the way. We recommend that you take advantage of the interpretive centers at Bear Meadow, Meta Lake, or Ryan Lake to learn more about Mt. St. Helens's changing environment. Bring shoes suitable for hiking on gravel trails.

After descending to Meta Lake, you can either continue climbing up to Windy Ridge for more unforgettable views and perhaps a snack at the Crater House Restaurant, or turn right on Highway 26 directly back to Iron Creek Campground. As the road descends back to the evergreen forests, you will see these from a new perspective, realizing how very delicate, beautiful, and miraculous a healthy ecosystem is. Like a near-death experience, you'll now carry in your memory a reference from which the vitality of life can be measured.

The Basics

Start: Iron Creek Campground, a pleasant 11-mile drive or bicycle ride from the town of Randle, located on Hwy. 12. From Randle, turn south onto Forest Service Rte. 25 at the Adams & St. Helens Restaurant, and follow it to the Iron Creek Campground turnoff. Halfway along this road is the Woods Creek Ranger Station, a good place to stop for additional information.

Length: 38 miles for the basic loop, or 54 miles if you ride all the way to Windy Ridge. Add 22 extra miles if you start bicycling in Randle.

Terrain: Mountainous, with steady climbs and sometimes narrow, winding roads.

Food: Take plenty to drink and eat for this challenging and often hot ride. Fresh water is available at Iron Creek Campground and

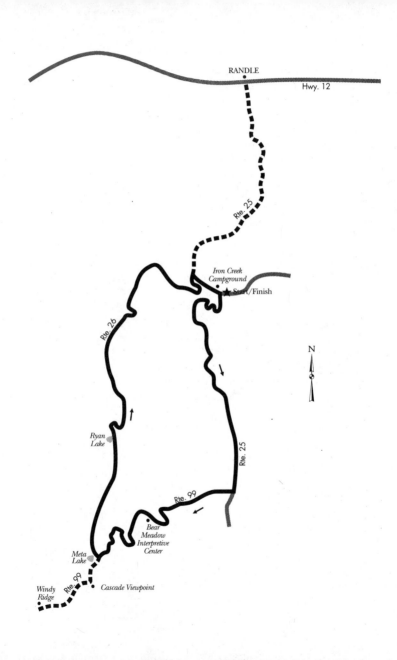

RANDLE

Hwy. 12

Rte. 25

Iron Creek
Campground

★ Start/Finish

Rte. 26

Ryan
Lake

Rte. 25

Rte. 99

Bear
Meadow
Interpretive
Center

Meta
Lake

Rte. 99

Windy
Ridge

Cascade Viewpoint

N

Meta Lake, at 19.5 miles. A small restaurant at the Cascade Viewpoint, about 2 miles past Meta Lake toward Windy Ridge, is the only place on this route to purchase food.

For more information: Randle Ranger Station, Randle, WA 98377; (360) 497–7565. Bicycle Adventures, P.O. Box 7875, Olympia, WA 98507; (800) 443–6060.

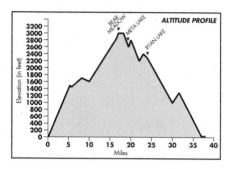

Miles & Directions

- 0.0 Turn left (south) on Forest Service Rte. 25. This is a fairly steady climb through the Gifford Pinchot National Forest.
- 10.0 Turn right onto Rte. 99. The intersection is well marked; just follow the signs to Mt. St. Helen's National Monument. The climbing continues.
- 17.0 Bear Meadow Interpretive Center and highest point on this ride.
- 19.5 Turn right on Rte. 26. Take this opportunity to see the Miner's Car Memorial and hike to Meta Lake.
  For more spectacular views, continue straight on Rte. 99 to Windy Ridge, 8 miles of winding and sometimes steep riding. The Crater House Restaurant at the Cascade Viewpoint is about 2.0 miles from Meta Lake.
- 24.0 Ryan Lake Interpretive Center, with trails and rest rooms.
- 37.0 Turn right on Rte. 25.
- 38.0 Return to Iron Creek Campground.

48

Fort Columbia Cruise

Fort Columbia—Chinook—Ilwaco
Willapa Refuge—Naselle—Fort Columbia

This ride offers bicyclists an opportunity to explore historic communities along the lower Columbia River, the Willapa National Wildlife Refuge, and inland timber areas. The ride starts at beautiful Fort Columbia State Park on the bank of the mighty Columbia River. The fort was constructed in 1898. For fifty years it defended the Columbia from foreign invaders. None ever came. Much of the fort is now maintained in its nineteenth-century condition for visitors to enjoy, and some of the buildings are used as dorms by the Washington chapter of American Youth Hostels. It is a popular stop for long-distance bicycle tourists riding the Pacific Coast.

As you ride, keep in mind some of the important events that occurred here at the mouth of the Columbia. In 1792 Capt. Robert Gray crossed the difficult bar into the river, establishing American claims to the Pacific Northwest. The British explorer Capt. George Vancouver had passed by earlier but had not seen the river. Late in 1805 Lewis and Clark completed their overland journey here.

Leaving the fort you'll follow the Columbia River westward through Chinook, a small community famous for its salmon fishing. During the late 1800s this was one of the wealthiest communities in the United States, thanks to more than one hundred fish traps in the river just off this beach. Fish traps were huge mechanical waterwheels that caught fish in giant buckets as they swam upriver to spawn. Each trap caught tons of salmon annually. Although fish traps were outlawed in 1935, the Chinook Packing Company on the west side of town still processes fish. The display standing in front of the fire hall describes this local history.

The Sea Resources Hatchery Complex, ½ mile north on Houchen Street, is Washington's oldest salmon hatchery. It was built in 1895 and continues to supply young salmon to augment natural fish runs. Call (360) 777–8229 if you would like a tour of the facility.

It's a pleasant ride to Ilwaco, a bustling town at the base of Cape Disappointment. The Ilwaco Heritage Museum (115 SE Lake Street) in the old Ilwaco Railroad Depot provides information about the region's history and traditional industries of fishing, logging, and cranberry farming. Exhibits describe the life of the Chinook people who populated the area before the intrusion of white settlers. In the days of steam ferries and railroads, Ilwaco was a major transportation link between Oregon and Washington. A 50-foot model of the peninsula includes a miniature "Clamshell Railroad," which once brought tourists from Oregon.

A worthwhile detour 3 miles farther west is Fort Canby State Park. There you'll see two lighthouses: North Head facing the Pacific and Cape Disappointment facing the Columbia River to the south. Shifting sandbars at the Columbia's mouth create a maritime hazard that has caused the wreck of more than two hundred ships over the last two centuries, including one ship bringing supplies to build the original light in 1853. It was once common to see ships sitting aground on the bars, hoping and waiting for a favorable tide to float off. Lt. Charles Wilkes, who led a mapping expedition in 1841, wrote, "Mere description can give little idea of the terrors of the bar. All who have seen it have spoken of the wildness of the scene and the incessant roar of the waters, representing it as one of the most fearful sights that can possibly meet the eye." What sailors describe as fearful, bicyclists can now enjoy as a spectacular view from the security of the lighthouses. An interpretive center at the fort includes a description of the Lewis and Clark Expedition.

From Ilwaco you'll ride north to the tourist town of Seaview, then turn east to continue on Highway 101. This curves north, where you'll pass the Willapa Wildlife Refuge. The refuge is an important stopping site for migrating birds and the year-round home for waterbirds and marine life. You can get more information about the refuge at the main office, at mile 21.3.

You'll turn off Highway 101 just before a sweeping bridge across the Naselle River. Follow quiet Parpala Road parallel to the river through a beautiful valley of radiant green farms and forests. It's a hilly but enjoyable stretch of roadway to Highway 401. Before turning south on the highway, you may want to detour 1 mile north to visit the Finnish-American community of Naselle.

It's an easy ride back to the Columbia River. Follow the highway past the Astoria Bridge, where Highway 401 merges into Highway 101. Just before you reach Fort Columbia State Park, the highway passes through a tunnel. For your safety there is a special flashing light to alert drivers that a bicyclist is riding through.

The Basics

Start: Fort Columbia State Park, on Hwy. 101, 2.5 miles west of the Astoria Bridge over the Columbia River.

Length: 45 or 38.7 miles.

Terrain: Some rolling hills.

Food: Stores and restaurants in Chinook, at 2 miles; Ilwaco at 8.5 miles; and Naselle, a 1-mile detour at 30.3 miles.

For more information: Contact the Fort Columbia Youth Hostel at (360) 777–8755.

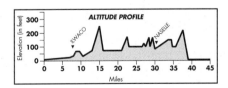

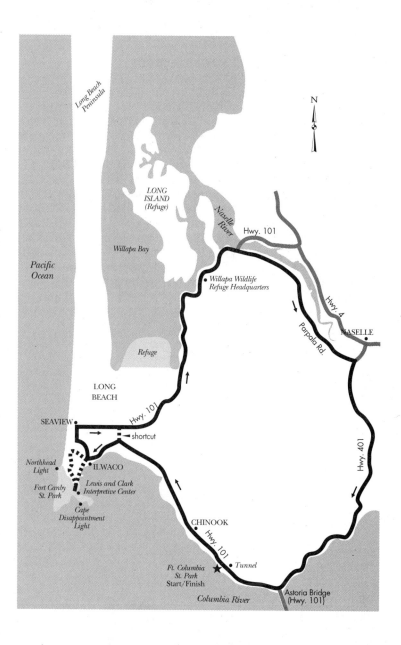

Miles & Directions

- 0.0 Head west on Hwy. 101.
- 2.0 Pass through the town of Chinook.
- 6.5 Continue straight toward Ilwaco. For a shortcut that avoids the traffic congestion of Ilwaco, turn right and rejoin the route at mile 12.8.
- 8.5 Turn right on 1st Ave. in Ilwaco, following Hwy. 101.
- 10.5 Turn right in Seaview to stay on Hwy. 101.
- 12.8 Continue straight (shortcut rejoins here).
- 23.3 Turn right on Parpala Rd., just before the Naselle River bridge.
- 30.3 Turn right onto Hwy. 401 (the town of Naselle, with stores and restaurants, is 1.0 mile to the left).
- 42.4 Continue straight onto Hwy. 101, past the Astoria Bridge.
- 44.7 Tunnel. Push button to start flashing lights that warn drivers of bicyclists.
- 45.0 End back at Fort Columbia.

49

Long Beach Peninsula Ramble

Seaview—Long Beach—Ocean Park
Oysterville—Nahcotta—Seaview

The Long Beach Peninsula has been a popular resort area for more than one hundred years. Its many miles of sandy ocean beaches, numerous tourist activities, and wildlife refuges attract visitors from all over the Northwest. Many bring their bicycles. This ride, popular with bicyclists of all abilities, provides an excellent overview of the peninsula's attractions.

You'll begin by riding through the communities of Seaview and Long Beach on Pacific Avenue, which is lined with gift shops, restaurants, and amusement rides. Wide sidewalks are crowded with vacationers, especially during the busy summer season. Pacific is a festive road where you can explore Marsh's Free Museum ("See Jake the Alligator Man; A Shrunken Head; The Two Headed Pig"), pass a monument marking the northwesternmost destination of the Lewis and Clark Expedition, and browse for antiques. There is always something going on in Long Beach; annual events include the Ragtime Rhodie Dixieland Jazz Festival in April, Sand-Sations Sand Sculpture Contest in July, and the International Kite Festival in August.

The highway out of town is straight and flat, allowing bicyclists to make good time. Traffic, including plenty of monster RVs, is congested for the first few miles but thins as you go north. The highway is shielded from the ocean by dunes, but there are many opportunities to stop at public beaches along the way north. From March through May visitors can often see gray whales migrating north offshore. Choose a cliff or other elevated spot to watch for a "spout" when one of the leviathans exhales. Whales usually travel in groups, so once you locate one you are likely to spot more.

At the beachfront community of Surfside, you'll turn east on Oysterville Road to cross the peninsula. You can take an enjoyable 3-mile side trip to windswept Leadbetter Point State Park, a popular destination for nature lovers. Much of the park is covered with stunted evergreen trees. The open dune area at the tip of the point is part of the Willapa National Wildlife Refuge, managed by the U.S. Fish and Wildlife Service. You'll find miles of sandy hiking trails and beaches to explore, plus plenty of good picnic spots. April and May are especially exciting times to visit, when thousands of birds stop at Leadbetter Point during their annual migration north. This is the northern breeding range of the snowy plover, which nests in the sand on the upper ocean beach from April through August.

Oysterville Road ends at a Willapa Bay beach that overlooks acres of oyster beds. During low tide you'll see workers out on the mud processing and harvesting the oysters. Oysterville, listed in the National Register of Historic Places, was once a bustling community. It was founded in the late 1850s by white settlers who harvested abundant local oysters to ship to San Francisco. By the 1880s the native oyster beds were decimated by overharvesting (the oysters now being grown are primarily the larger Japanese variety). For several years Oysterville was the county seat, but residents from other parts of Pacific County resented having to travel to the end of the railroad line to transact official business. Now it's a quiet village. You'll enjoy strolling along the streets of beautiful Victorian-era homes, visiting the restored 1892 Baptist church (now a historic museum), or just watching the breeze blow over Willapa Bay.

If you've worked up an appetite by the time you pass through the small community of Nahcotta, you're in for a treat. The famous Ark Restaurant and Bakery offers some of the best in Northwest cuisine, especially if you like seafood. If you can't eat now, pick up a copy of *The Ark Restaurant Cookbook,* in which chefs Jimella Lucas and Nanci Main share recipes that include Scallops Nectarine, Sturgeon with Garlic Raspberry Sauce, and Cranberry Butter.

The cranberries used in these recipes are probably grown locally. As you ride you may notice reddish green plants growing beyond the road in low beds flooded with fresh water: cranberry bogs. These tart berries were first grown commercially in 1881 along Cranberry Road. Handpicking once employed many of the local residents. An agricultural extension station on the peninsula helped develop mechanical techniques that have made harvesting easier, and cranberries continue to represent a major crop in this area. More than five hundred acres on the Long Beach Peninsula are planted in cranberries, representing about half of the total crop grown in Washington State.

Sandridge Road takes you south along the Willapa Bay shoreline. Looking east you'll see Long Island, considered the largest estuarine island on the Pacific Coast. This is part of the Willapa National Wildlife Refuge, an important wildlife sanctuary with abundant evergreen plants and animals (more than two hundred varieties of birds) in the protected forests and wetlands. Long Island has a 274-acre grove of red cedars, one of the last remaining stands of this unique climax ecosystem. Access is unrestricted, provided you have a boat to reach the island.

The Basics

Start: Seaview Tourist Information Center, at the corner of Hwy. 101 and Pacific Ave. For a shorter, easier loop around the north end of the peninsula, begin at Ocean Park, 11 miles north.

Length: 32.7 miles; or 11 miles starting from Ocean Park.

Terrain: Almost entirely flat. Traffic can be heavy at the southern end of the peninsula during the tourist season.

Food: There is a wide variety in Seaview and Long Beach; stores and restaurants in Ocean Park, at 11 miles; store in Oysterville, at

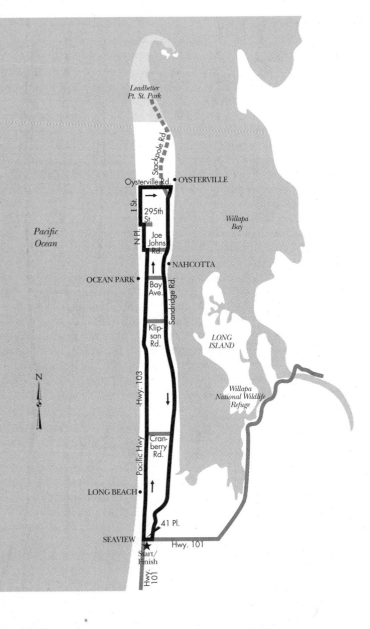

16 miles; a store and the famous Ark Restaurant are at Nahcotta.
For more information: Long Beach Peninsula Visitors Bureau,
P.O. Box 562, Long Beach, WA 98631; (800) 451–2542.

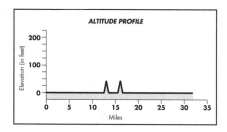

Miles & Directions

- 0.0 North on Pacific Ave. (Hwy. 103).
- 11.0 Continue straight at stop-sign intersection in Ocean Park.
- 12.5 Turn left on Joe Johns Rd., then a quick right onto N Pl.
- 12.8 Left on 295th, over a dune toward the beach.
- 13.0 Right onto I St.
- 15.3 Right onto Oysterville Rd.
- 16.5 Take the last right turn before Willapa Bay. This takes you through Oysterville, past the old schoolhouse and Baptist church.
- 17.1 Merge left onto Sandridge Rd.
- 20.3 Nahcotta. The Ark Restaurant is to the left. For short loop, turn right at Bay Ave. to return to Ocean Park.
- 32.1 Right onto 41 Pl, just before Hwy. 101 stop sign.
- 32.5 Left on N Pl, then right onto Hwy. 101.
- 32.7 End back at the Seaview Tourist Information Center.

50

Gunderson Loop Cruise

Forks—Olympic National Forest—Forks

Forks, Washington, is located on the isolated and beautiful Pacific coast side of the Olympia Peninsula. The region is covered by a hilly patchwork of forests and clear-cuts, evidence of the timber industry that has long been the lifeblood of the community's economy. Forks called itself the "Forestry Capital of the World." Overdependence on a single industry has become an economic liability, however, so the community has diversified into new sectors.

Shirley and Lew McGill are doing their part by promoting another use of the forested hills: mountain biking. Their Olympic Mountains Bike Shop, located in downtown Forks at 78 South A Street, is one of the most accommodating and friendly bike shops you'll find. The McGills' enthusiasm is contagious. If you need a bicycle, they'll gladly rent you a quality steed. If you brought your won, they'll offer directions and advice for an enjoyable adventure.

There is a full menu to choose from in the Forks area. The region is crisscrossed with dirt roads and trails that range from leisurely to lunatic. The route described here, Gunderson Loop, is an easy ride on well-maintained logging roads and abandoned railroad lines. It is ideal for a beginning off-road bicyclist, and is even suitable for towing a trailer. Riders who desire greater challenges should stop by the McGills' shop or check out the Olympic National Forest information center a few miles north of Forks for local and current advice.

Take a few precautions when you bicycle in the forest. You'll need a suitable map and a compass. Even with these in hand, it is *extremely* easy to get lost when riding on unfamiliar mountain roads and trails (there are generally no signposts), so be sure to hone your navigation skills before exploring new territory. Conditions can change quickly, so always be prepared with sufficient water, snacks, extra clothes, rain gear, and emergency equipment to handle unexpected situations.

Never ride so fast that you can't stop for other trail users. Bicyclists are required to yield to hikers and equestrians. Try not to frighten horses. It is usually best to stop and get completely off the trail so they can walk by. Maintaining good relations with other trail users helps prevent future restrictions on bicycle use.

Be sure to schedule time to explore Forks while you are there. About a half mile south of town on Highway 101 is the Forks Visitors Center and Timber Museum, where you can learn about the community's heritage. There is a friendly downtown business district with plenty of cafés where you can rub shoulders with seasoned timber workers over flapjacks and coffee. The public transit system accommodates bicycles with nifty racks on buses from Port Angles and Sequim, so you can now visit Forks without taking your car: Bicycle one way and get a lift back. For information call Clallam Transit at (360) 452–4511.

The Basics

Start: Tillicum Park on Forks Ave. (Hwy. 101) just north of downtown.

Length: 18.6 miles.

Terrain: The first and last stretch follows Hwy. 101, which has a wide and well-paved shoulder. Once off the highway you'll ride on relatively well-maintained and level gravel roads. As with any unpaved road, expect mud when it rains and dust when it's hot.

Food: Except for a restaurant and tavern on the highway north of town, there are no opportunities to buy food along this route so be sure to bring your own.

For more information: Olympic Mountain Bike Shop, 78 South A Street, Forks, WA 98331; (360) 374–4321. Forks Visitor Information, 1411 S. Forks Ave., P.O. Box 1249, Forks, WA 98331, (360) 374–2531 or (800) 44 FORKS.

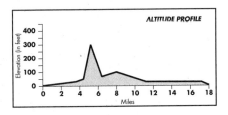

Miles & Directions

- 0.0 Turn right from Tillicum Park onto Forks Ave. N. (Hwy. 101).
- 3.5 Turn left onto gravel road D2000 (about 0.2 mile past mile marker 195).
- 5.4 Optional turnoff on left to lookout (about 400-foot climb) at top of hill.
- 6.4 Turn left onto Rd. D4000.
- 6.6 Bear right.
- 11.5 Turn left onto gravel road. Ride past lumber mill yards.
- 14.0 Cross river on cement bridge, then turn left on gravel road.
- 15.0 Bear right as directed. The road becomes paved in 0.2 mile.
- 17.2 Turn right on Hwy. 101.
- 18.6 End back at Tillicum Park.

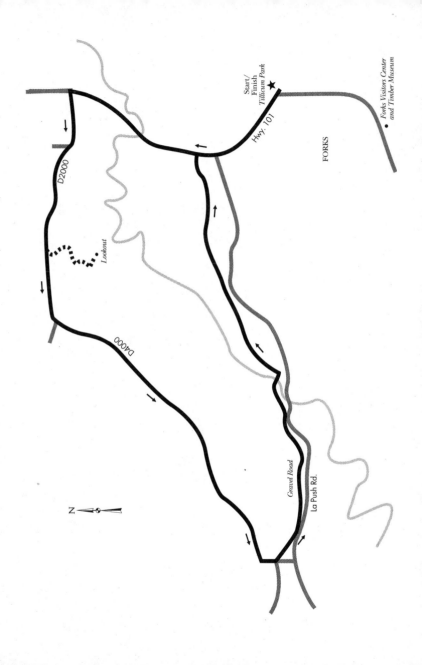

Appendix

There are a number of resources that can help you enjoy our many-faceted sport. We especially recommend three:

■ **Your local bicycling club.** Your club keeps you informed about local cycling activities, supports bicycling in your community, and lets you meet others who share your interest. Contact a good local bicycle shop or your city recreation department for information about bicycle clubs in your area.

■ **Regional cycling magazines.** These provide a calendar of cycling events and information about regional cycling issues. In the Northwest these include *Oregon Cycling* and *The Bicycle Paper.*

■ **The League of American Bicyclists** or **The Canadian Cycling Association.** These national bicycling organizations provide a variety of unique services and represent your political interests at the national level.

Below are the addresses of these and other useful organizations.

Bicycling Organizations

Adventure Cycling Association
P.O. Box 8308
Missoula, MT 59807
(406) 721–1776

Nonprofit organization for long-distance bicycle touring. Provides a variety of resources and services.

American Youth Hostels
P.O. Box 37613
Washington, DC 20013
(202) 783–6161

Manages more than 200 hostels in North America. Local chapters sponsor cycling trips and events.

Cycling British Columbia
332 1367 W. Broadway
Vancouver, BC V6H 4A9
(604) 737–3034
Provincial bicycling organization promotes racing, touring, and safety.

Canadian Cycling Association
1600 James Naismith Dr.
Gloucester, ON K1B 5N4
(613) 748–5629

Institute for Transportation
and Development Policy
611 Broadway, Room 616
New York, NY 10012
(212) 260–8144
Promotes bicycling and other socially and environmentally responsible forms of transportation throughout the world.

International Bicycle Fund
4887 Columbia Dr. S.
Seattle, WA 98108
(206) 628–9314
Promotes bicycle transportation and bicycle safety education in North America and throughout the world.

League of American Bicyclists
190 W. Ostend St., Suite 120
Baltimore, MD 21230
(410) 539–3399
National organization of bicyclists. Supports a variety of member services for individuals and clubs. Publishes *Bicycle USA* magazine and an annual almanac of bicycling resources.

Rails-to-Trails Conservancy
1400 Sixteenth St. NW
Washington, D.C. 20036
(202) 797–5400
National organization promotes the development of public trails from abandoned railroad rights-of-way.

Touring Exchange
P.O. Box 265
Port Townsend, WA 98368
(360) 385–0667
Collects and sells bicycle route information.

Victoria Transport Policy Institute
1250 Rudlin St.
Victoria, BC V8V 3R7
Phone and fax: (250) 360–1560

Performs research on ways to provide transportation with positive environmental and social impacts, including bicycle and pedestrian encouragement.

Regional Cycling Magazines

The Bicycle Paper
1535 11th Ave.
Seattle, WA 98105

Covers racing, touring, and bicycling club activities and related issues in Washington and Oregon.

Oregon Cycling
544 W. 1st Ave.
Eugene, OR 97401

Covers touring, recreational cycling, and advocacy in Oregon.

Tourism Offices

These agencies provide visitor information. Some have materials specifically for bicyclists.

British Columbia Ministry of Tourism
Parliament Buildings
Victoria, BC V8V 1X4
(800) 663–6000 or
(250) 387–1642

Idaho Travel Council
Capitol Building, Room 108
700 W. State St.
Boise, ID 83707
(800) 635–7820 or
(208) 334–2470

Oregon Tourism Division
775 Summer St. NE
Salem, OR 97310
(800) 547–7842

Washington State Tourism Office
101 GA Building AX-13
Olympia, WA 98504
(800) 544–1800 or (360) 586–2088, general tourism information; (360) 705–7277, bicycle information

Bicycle Tour Companies

Backroads Tours
1516 5th St., A103
Berkeley, CA 94710
(800) 462–2848 or
(510) 527–1555

Bicycle Adventure
P.O Box 7875
Olympia, WA 98507
(800) 443–6060 or
(360) 786–0989

Bicycle Maps

Ada County Ridge to Rivers
Bikeway Map (free)
Ada Planning Association
413 W. Idaho, #100
Boise, ID 83702
(208) 345–5274

Biking Pierce County (free)
Pierce County Planning Department
2401 S. 35th St.
Tacoma, WA 98409

Eugene Bicycle Map (fee)
Bicycle Coordinator
858 Pearl St.
Eugene, OR 97401
(541) 687–5298

Idaho State Bicycle Map (free)
Bicycle Coordinator
Idaho Department of Trans-
portation
P.O. Box 7129
Boise, ID 83707-1129
(208) 334–8296

King County Parks and Recreation Map (fee)
King County Natural Re-
sources and Parks Division
2040 84th Ave. SE
Mercer Island, WA 98040

Methow Valley Mountain
Bike Guide (fee)
Winthrop Ranger District
P.O. Box 579
Winthrop, WA 98862
(509) 996–2266

Oregon Bicycling Guide and Oregon Coast Bike Route Map (free)
Bikeway Program Manager
Oregon Department of Transportation
Salem, OR 97310
(503) 986–3555

Portland Metro Area Bicycle Map (fee)
Bicycle and Pedestrian Program
1120 SW 5th Ave., #834
Portland, OR 97204

Sea-Tac Airport to Downtown Seattle and Seattle Bicycle Guidemap (free)
Bicycle Program
Seattle Engineering Department
708 Municipal Building
600 Fourth Ave.
Seattle, WA 98104
(206) 684–7583

About the Authors

Suzanne Kort and Todd Litman are experienced bicyclists who enjoy club rides, bicycle commuting, and touring. Together they have ridden by tandem bicycle across the Pacific Northwest and Western Canada. They now tow a bicycle trailer with their two sons, Graham and Raviv.

Todd is a transportation economist and policy analyst. He directs the Victoria Transport Policy Institute, which performs research on the social and environmental impacts of transportation. Todd has worked as a bike-shop manager, bicycle tour leader, bicycle safety instructor, and bicycle journalist. He has served as officer of local, state, and national bicycling organizations, and was a lobbyist for the Bicycle Federation of Washington.

Suzanne is a full-time mother and published poet with a degree in environmental science. She is editor and research assistant for the Victoria Transport Policy Institute. She has worked as a field biologist, environmental chemist, technical writer, massage practitioner, and educator. Suzanne and Todd are married and live in Victoria, British Columbia.

Acknowledgments

This book would not exist without the considerable help and encouragement of many wonderful people. Every bicycle-club volunteer whose ride appears in these pages has contributed toward this book, as have countless store clerks, restaurant staff, and public officials who provided food, shelter, and information during our long and sometimes difficult scouting trips. It is not possible to list everybody who deserves our appreciation and recognition, but we would like to express special thanks to a few: Duane and Linda Adams, Lopez Island; Maya Alsop, Bellingham; Deirdre Arscott, Vancouver; Dan Baris, Yakima; Bob, Steve, and Rick of Bicycling Adventures, Olympia; Diane Bishop, Eugene; Chris Brandmein, Lopez Island; Canden Brewster; Mark and Jean Chinn, Medford; Kathy Duden Davies, Seattle; Dave Hagen, Lewiston; John Ittner, Bob and Patsy King, BIKES; Peter Lagerway, Seattle; Jim Lazar, Olympia; Danelle Laidlaw, Vancouver; Diane Lister, Tacoma Wheelmen; Belinda McMillen, Ellensberg; Phil Miller, King Co.; Richard Moffit, Springfield; Peter Murray, Vashon Island; Mary Norton, Snoqualmie; Dave Olson; Malcolm Parry, Pendleton; Ken Seymour, Pullman; Don Shaffer, Salem; Margaret Slack, Fort Langely; C. Douglas Smith, Vancouver; Connie Smithisley; Harry Stavert, Marysville; Steven Stewart, Aloha; Fred Strong, NBTS; Sybil Suthergreen, Seattle; Allen and Janet Throop, Corvallis; Jim Tow, Tri-Cities; Carol Vanetta, Seattle; Tim Wahl, Bellingham; Bob Watson, Walla Walla; David Whitman, Bickleton; Michael Wolfe, Salem; Margaret Watson and Spokane's Golden Girls, who demonstrated a wonderful ability to combine bicycling with fun, friendship, and wisdom.